Comments on other *Amazing Stories* from readers & reviewers

"Tightly written volumes filled with lots of wit and humour about famous and infamous Canadians."
Eric Shackleton, *The Globe and Mail*

"The heightened sense of drama and intrigue, combined with a good dose of human interest is what sets Amazing Stories *apart."*
Pamela Klaffke, *Calgary Herald*

"This is popular history as it should be... For this price, buy two and give one to a friend."
Terry Cook, a reader from Ottawa, on **Rebel Women**

"Glasner creates the moment of the explosion itself in graphic detail...she builds detail upon gruesome detail to create a convincingly authentic picture."
Peggy McKinnon, *The Sunday Herald,* on **The Halifax Explosion**

"It was wonderful...I found I could not put it down. I was sorry when it was completed."
Dorothy F. from Manitoba on **Marie-Anne Lagimodière**

"Stories are rich in description, and bristle with a clever, stylish realness."
Mark Weber, *Central Alberta Advisor,* on **Ghost Town Stories II**

"A compelling read. Bertin...has selected only the most intriguing tales, which she narrates with a wealth of detail."
Joyce Glasner, *New Brunswick Reader,* on **Strange Events**

"The resulting book is one readers will want to share with all the women in their lives."
Lynn Martel, *Rocky Mountain Outlook,* on **Women Explorers**

AMAZING STORIES®

DEADLY WOMEN OF ONTARIO

AMAZING STORIES®

DEADLY WOMEN OF ONTARIO

Murderous Tales of Deceit and Treachery

HISTORY/CRIME

by Cheryl MacDonald

PUBLISHED BY ALTITUDE PUBLISHING CANADA LTD.
1500 Railway Avenue, Canmore, Alberta T1W 1P6
www.altitudepublishing.com
1-800-957-6888

Extreme care has been taken to ensure that all information presented in
this book is accurate and up to date. Neither the author nor the
publisher can be held responsible for any errors.

Publisher	Stephen Hutchings
Associate Publisher	Kara Turner
Editor	Deborah Lawson
Digital Photo Colouring	Bryan Pezzi

We acknowledge the financial support of the Government
of Canada through the Book Publishing Industry Development
Program (BPIDP) for our publishing activities.

Altitude GreenTree Program
Altitude Publishing will plant twice as many trees as were used
in the manufacturing of this product.

National Library of Canada Cataloguing in Publication Data

MacDonald, Cheryl, 1952-
Deadly women of Ontario / Cheryl MacDonald.

(Amazing stories)
ISBN 1-55439-026-5

1. Women murders--Ontario--Biography. I. Title. II. Series: Amazing stories (Calgary, Alta.)

HV6805.M27 2005   364.1'523'0922713   C2005-902841-6

Amazing Stories® is a registered trademark of Altitude Publishing Canada Ltd.

Printed and bound in Canada by Friesens
2 4 6 8 9 7 5 3 1

For my very good friend Dana B. Stavinga —
the "deadliest" woman in Haldimand County

Contents

b

Prologue

April 16, 1911 was Easter Sunday. When Pietro Napolitano made his way home from a night shift at the Sault Ste. Marie steel mill, he was in his usual foul mood. Pietro was bone-tired and disgusted. He was convinced he had to work harder than anyone else for half as much. He hated the house he and his 28-year-old wife Angelina rented in Little Italy, the immigrant enclave in "the Soo's" west end. What Pietro wanted was his own house, like the one he had owned in Thessalon, Ontario. But it took money to buy a house and nearly all of Pietro's money went to support his family. Now, if Angelina would do as she was told and earn some money, things would be different.

By the time he walked through the door of the rented house, Pietro had worked himself into a fury over Angelina's defiance. Soon, neighbours heard the familiar sound of the Napolitanos screaming furiously at each other.

At noon, Pietro went upstairs to bed. Angelina stayed downstairs. She'd had enough. The time for words was past. Now was the time for action. An hour later Angelina climbed the stairs, a little more slowly than usual because she was six months pregnant with her fifth child. But the baby wasn't the only extra weight Angelina carried. In her hands was an axe she had taken from the garden shed moments before. She entered the bedroom she shared with Pietro. Her husband was sound asleep, oblivious to her presence.

Angelina raised the axe and struck Pietro in the head — once, twice, then again and again.

Chapter 1
Mary Osborn: "Get the Old Rascal Out of the Way"

R unning a farm was extremely hard work in the colonial period, but following the American Revolution many residents of the new United States moved to Upper Canada, lured by promises of good land. One of them was Bartholomew London. Originally from New Jersey, he was imprisoned there during the American Revolution. In 1789, when he was close to 60, he left his wife behind and moved to the area around Lake Ontario with four children and four grandchildren. They settled in Saltfleet Township — now Stoney Creek — near the shores of Lake Ontario.

A smoothly run farm required an extensive household, including an experienced woman to oversee the henhouse, dairy, and domestic chores. Bartholomew eventually hired a housekeeper, Mary Osborn.

Mary was from Pennsylvania. A widow with two sons, she was in her twenties, more than 40 years younger than Bartholomew. Despite their age difference, the two became intimate. When Mary was found to be pregnant, Bartholomew married her. Their daughter Hannah was born on April 5, 1799.

According to the *Niagara Herald,* one of the few news-papers published in the province at the time, the first Mrs. London was still alive then. However, Bartholomew's second marriage was not that unusual. Divorce was out of reach for most people well into the twentieth century. In the 1800s, when transportation was slow and communication irregular, a man or woman who wanted to marry a second time could simply move far away from an unwanted spouse and form another relationship.

Regardless of any legal irregularities that may have existed, Bartholomew recognized Mary as his wife. On May 4, 1800 he changed his will in her favour. After bequeath-ing various sums of money to his own sons, he left the bulk of his estate in the hands of "my beloved wife Marey." Bartholomew instructed that Mary use the inheritance to raise her sons, as well as their daughter Hannah and any other children Bartholomew might father. If she remarried, Mary would retain a third of the estate, a very generous settlement at a time when men routinely wrote wills that left their widows with nothing if they were to remarry. Clearly, Bartholomew was besotted with Mary.

But it seems she did not return his feelings. When George Nemiers, another Pennsylvanian, arrived to work on the London farm, he and Mary became lovers. Rumour claimed that the pair had been acquainted in Pennsylvania. In hindsight, it is difficult not to wonder whether Mary and George had planned to reunite after she had ensured a secure financial future for herself and her children.

By the late fall of 1800 Mary was pregnant again. She did not know who the father was, but the pregnancy may have forced her to take action. She and George decided to kill Bartholomew. According to Mary, it was George who first proposed that they "get the old rascal out of the way, and the sooner it was done the better." Mary suggested shooting him, but George rejected that option.

A short time later, a violent quarrel erupted between Mary and her husband. Possibly it was staged, although Mary later claimed it was all George's fault. In any event, while Bartholomew was fighting with Mary, George came to her rescue, hitting his employer on the head with a shoe hammer and fracturing his skull.

The injury was serious but Bartholomew was a tough character. He survived and there seemed to be a good chance he would recover. Mary and George lost patience and decided to poison him.

George was given the task of procuring the poison and

made a trip to Ancaster, west of Hamilton, to do so. He lost his nerve, however, and returned home empty-handed. A second trip, this one to Canadaigua, New York, proved more successful. He obtained two ounces of "ratsbane" — otherwise known as arsenic — along with an ounce of opium. Some time in early February 1801, Mary served Bartholomew two doses of arsenic-laced whiskey. According to a later newspaper report, both drinks "brought on a puking without further injury." Then, on February 16, Mary gave Bartholomew a third dose of whiskey and arsenic. This time the concoction proved fatal and Bartholomew died on February 17.

But neighbourhood suspicions had been aroused. Authorities were alerted immediately after Bartholomew's death, and they performed an autopsy. The physicians involved, including Dr. Oliver Tiffany, agreed that the cause of death had been poisoning. Mary Osborn and George Nemiers were taken into custody.

Under normal circumstances, the trial would have taken place at the spring assizes, one of the periodic sessions of court that heard cases beyond the jurisdiction of local justices of the peace. However, Mary's pregnancy delayed proceedings until August. Her second daughter, Catherine, was born on August 9. On Friday, August 14, five days after her daughter was born, Mary and George were in court at Newark (now known as Niagara-on-the-Lake), the capital of the District of Niagara, which then included Saltfleet Township.

The trial began at 8:30 in the morning and lasted eight hours. Henry Allcock, one of the most powerful men in the province, presided, along with associate justices Robert Hamilton, a wealthy Scottish businessman, and William Dickson. Jury members included other influential Niagara residents, among them merchants John Dun and James Crooks. A total of 14 witnesses were called, including Dr. Oliver Tiffany, newspaper publisher Silvester Tiffany, and Dr. Robert Kerr, from whom George Nemiers had originally tried to obtain arsenic.

The evidence presented was circumstantial. While there was no doubt in the minds of medical experts that Bartholomew London had died of poison, there was no proof as to who had administered it. However, during the six months they'd spent in jail, George and Mary had flung accusations at each other. It became clear that, no matter who had initiated the plot and given the poison, both of them had wanted to see Bartholomew dead.

Mary Osborn and George Nemiers were convicted and sentenced to hang "until they be dead, dead, and afterwards their bodies to be Dissected," in accordance with the common practice of the day to turn over the bodies of executed criminals to doctors for medical research.

The legal system moved quickly in those days. The executions were set for the following Monday, August 17. In the interval, Silvester Tiffany visited the condemned pair in their cells. He later described their behaviour and some of their comments in the *Herald*. George Nemiers, he reported, was remorseful. He told Tiffany he had been raised by decent, God-fearing parents who were in no way responsible for his crime. Instead, he laid the blame squarely on Mary, saying she had "lured him to unlawful intimacy and connection about nine months ago, and from the sin of adultery to that of murder."

George also made it clear that he was not interested in gaining control of Bartholomew's property. "It was not the estate, but the woman he wanted," wrote Tiffany. Although the publisher did not elaborate on this, it was an important point. The courts tended to deal most harshly with those convicted of crimes against their so-called betters, especially when potential financial gain led to violence. By killing his employer, presumably in the hope of marrying Mary and assuming control of the family farm, George had placed himself squarely in this category.

Even if George had been able to convince the jury that he had acted without thought of financial gain, it probably would not have saved him from the gallows. But he wanted it plainly known that his sole motive had been to remove the obstacle between himself and Mary.

George also claimed someone else had been involved, hinting that it was this person who had originally suggested killing Bartholomew. At first Mary refused to confirm this statement, telling George to be quiet, that "two of us to die for this is enough." But she eventually relented, and either George or Mary told Silvester Tiffany the name of the third individual.

Perhaps it was someone close to the newspaper publisher. Perhaps one of Bartholomew's grown children, hoping to obtain more land, had instigated the crime. Or perhaps a powerful member of Niagara District society had made a deal to get all or part of the London farm after Bartholomew's demise. Whoever it was, Tiffany chose not to reveal the information.

Was there really a third person involved in the murder of Bartholomew London? Or had Mary and George lied in order to confuse the issue and gain a bit more time?

According to the *Herald* publisher, Mary seemed unconvinced throughout the proceedings that she would actually be hanged. She gave only the barest details of her involvement in the crime until shortly before she and her lover were led to the gallows.

A large crowd gathered to watch on the morning of August 17. At least one of them, a woman, mocked Mary, imitating her gestures and expressions as she walked out before the witnesses. According to Silvester Tiffany, it wasn't until Mary was led to the scaffold and the rope was placed about her neck that she cried out, as though finally realizing she was going to hang.

Tiffany gave a few details about the pair's final moments. "When she came out to her place she said, 'May this be a warning to you all,' and prayed to God to have mercy on her soul. They remained silent for some time; the floor falling, launched them into eternity."

Mary Osborn was the first woman executed in Upper Canada.

Silvester Tiffany ended his account of the trial and execution with a moral lesson to readers, warning them that adultery could easily lead to murder. "There is visible in the whole of this business, the hand of Providence pursuing with vengeance offenders even in this life; for in it we see punished adultery, disregard of marriage vows, and murder: and to those who indulge themselves in the two former, it may be a lesson of instruction that from them to the last is but a step."

As for Mary's daughters, family tradition claims that Hannah was raised in the home of Bartholomew's grown daughter, Mehitable London Whitsell. Catherine, who may not have been Bartholomew's daughter but was legally recognized as such, was likely raised by another relative. She grew to adulthood, dying in May 1879 at Caistor Centre, less than an hour southwest of the farm where Bartholomew London had been murdered.

Chapter 2
Mary Aylward:
"May Almighty God
Increase His Pain!"

t the age of 12, Mary O'Brien left her home in Limerick County, Ireland, to emigrate to America. She reached New York and, like so many other young Irish Catholic girls, went into domestic service.

Mary grew into an attractive young woman with dark hair, fair skin, and bright eyes. In time she caught the attention of another young Irish immigrant. Richard Aylward was two years older and, like Mary, had arrived in the United States in about 1850.

Around 1855 the couple married and their first daughter was born soon afterwards. In time two more daughters followed. By 1862 the Aylwards were living on a farm in

Belleville, Ontario, and had settled into the rhythmic routine of the seasons. In May of that year Richard borrowed a scythe from a neighbour, William Munro, and took it to a fellow named McCrea to have it sharpened. Soon it would be haying season and Richard wanted to make sure he was prepared to harvest enough to feed his livestock.

On May 16 William Munro and his son, Alexander, called at the Aylward farm. Munro was looking for some of his hens, which had wandered off. The hens were a sore point with Richard Aylward, who did not want them eating his grain. In fact, the birds were just one of many causes of friction between him and his neighbour. Although they co-operated when necessary, sharing tools or exchanging labour in the time-honoured tradition of rural communities, Richard Aylward and William Munro were not on the best of terms.

This particular day, as Richard and the two Munros walked from the Aylward house to the field, their conversation centred on the hens. Richard, who was carrying a shotgun, told his neighbour that he had not shot any of Munro's hens yet, but he might if they continued getting into his grain.

William replied that he didn't care how many hens Richard shot — "as long as he did not carry them off." The implication was that by doing so, Richard would be stealing.

Richard Aylward was a nervous, high-strung man who became excited easily. The conversation quickly turned into a quarrel, and then a struggle. Suddenly, William Munro pulled out a pistol he was carrying.

Richard called for his wife. Mary grabbed the scythe and ran to his assistance. By the time she arrived, William Munro had been shot and was lying on the ground — wounded, but still alive. Fuelled by adrenaline and hatred of Munro, she struck him once with the scythe. Meanwhile, the fallen man had shouted to his son Alexander to pick up the pistol, which he had dropped in the scuffle. The boy, who was larger than Richard, tried to get his father's weapon, and then turned to flee. Richard shot him in the back.

Although the *Canadian Freeman* later reported that "26 slugs" were removed from Alexander Munro's back, in all probability the bullets were actually small pellets or birdshot. Alexander recovered quickly. His father was not so fortunate. After lingering for nearly two weeks, William Munro succumbed to his injuries. Shortly after word of his death reached Hastings County authorities, Mary and Richard Aylward were arrested for murder. They soon found themselves at the centre of a controversy fuelled by class and religious biases.

The Munros were relatively prosperous farmers, well established in the Belleville area. In contrast, the Aylwards were newcomers, and Irish Catholic to boot. Although Belleville had a sizeable Catholic population, most of whom attended St. Michael's Church, Irish Catholic immigrants were typically characterized as stubborn and hotheaded. This undercurrent of animosity and suspicion had its consequences.

Some of the witnesses at the October trial believed the Aylwards had been contemplating the murder of William Munro for some time. The testimony of Isabella McCrea, the wife of the man who sharpened the scythe for Richard Aylward, gave her insight into Mary's character. According to Isabella, Mary had talked freely about her hatred for William Munro and said she was going to kill him. All she needed to do was decide which weapon to use. Following the incident in the field, Mary had shown Isabella "Old Baldy's" hat, pointing out the spot where the scythe had struck him. Isabella also recalled that when Mary heard Munro was suffering from his wounds, the Irishwoman had fervently burst out, "May Almighty God increase his pain!"

Quite a fuss was made about the sharpening of the scythe. Although anyone familiar with farming knew that scythes were frequently used in late spring, the prosecution suggested Richard had deliberately sharpened the blade with the intention of using it as a weapon.

The jurors faced a curious discrepancy between Alexander Munro's testimony and that of another witness, John House. As far as Alexander was concerned, the Aylwards had attacked William without provocation. But House put a slightly different spin on things. He recalled that, although William Munro had been perfectly lucid in the days between the altercation at the Aylwards' farm and his death, he had repeatedly refused to lay charges against his attackers, even when his family and friends pressed him to do so. According to House, William had said "he had no business interfering with them." In House's mind, it seemed clear that William Munro believed the whole unfortunate episode had been his own fault. But Alexander Munro said he had never heard his father make such a statement, and there were many who believed the son of the slain man.

There was no doubt that there had been a fight. There was no doubt that Richard Aylward had shot both William and Alexander or that Mary had struck the blow that ultimately killed William. The question was, had murder been committed? Under British common law, a man did have the right to defend his property. If Richard Aylward had felt threatened, no murder had been committed. But if Richard had been the aggressor and Mary had come to his aid, both would be found guilty of murder.

For many residents of Belleville and the surrounding area, the outcome of the trial was a foregone conclusion. The Munros had standing in the community and a number of powerful friends. The Aylwards were struggling new arrivals, most of whose friends were in similar circumstances. In fact, at least one neighbour was too poor to afford the expense involved in making a journey to Belleville to testify for the defence. Long before the verdict was reached, people were saying to Father Brennen, the priest at St. Michael's Roman Catholic Church, "Aylward and his wife are doomed."

Their predictions proved true. Mary and Richard were found guilty. Although the jury recommended mercy, the judge was compelled to follow the law and had no choice but to sentence them to hang. Their execution was scheduled for December 8.

Objecting that the Aylwards were victims of anti-Catholic, anti-Irish feeling, sympathizers sent petitions asking that their death sentences be changed to prison terms. But the Munros also had sympathizers whose influence turned out to be stronger. When it became apparent that the Department of Justice would not stop the executions, a direct appeal was made to the governor-general, Viscount Charles Stanley Monck, who, like the Aylwards, had been born in Ireland. He refused to intervene.

As the day for the execution drew near, hundreds of visitors poured into Belleville. Many gathered outside the courthouse on December 7 and stayed there overnight, risking frostbitten toes and noses in order to get a glimpse of the condemned couple. The scaffold was already in place, erected so the platform was level with a second-storey window. Two trap doors had been built, about three feet apart. Above them was a long beam into which had been inserted two strong steel hooks, each centred above a trap door.

December 8 dawned clear and cool, although clouds covered the sky soon after daybreak. The crowd waited anxiously. Ten o'clock came and went, with no sign of the prisoners. There were rumours that a last-minute telegram was expected from Ottawa. None came. Finally, at eleven o'clock, the hangman stepped out of the second-floor window onto the scaffold, followed by officials. Then Richard Aylward appeared. Handcuffs pinned his hands behind his back and a rope had already been placed about his neck. Father Brennen came next, followed by Mary. Like Richard, she was manacled. She was dressed entirely in white, with a crepe shawl around her shoulders. Behind her came Father Lawlor, another priest from St. Michael's.

Mary and Richard looked pale and frightened. After the warrant was read, the ropes were attached to the overhead hooks. Father Brennen began a prayer. Both the Aylwards fell to their knees on top of the trap doors. The priest asked Richard if he had anything to say, but the young man was unable to speak. Father Brennen asked the crowd to pray for their souls. As he continued to pray, Mary and Richard joined in. Before they were finished the hangman pulled the lever, opening the trap doors. Their bodies dropped. Father Brennen fainted.

Mary died instantly. Richard's struggle seemed to go on for an eternity, but actually lasted less than three minutes. Officials left their bodies suspended for about half an hour, then cut them down. After a final examination, the earthly remains of Mary and Richard Aylward were placed in two caskets, then taken to St. Michael's Church and placed in the central aisle.

As convicted murderers, the Aylwards might have been denied burial in consecrated ground. However, soon after he began the funeral Mass at three o'clock that afternoon, Father

Brennen announced he considered the Aylwards innocent. The sermon he delivered to the packed church was basically a review of the case. "They were never guilty of the crimes for which they died," Brennen declared. Item by item, he went over the events that had led to the executions. By the time he was finished many of his listeners were weeping.

Richard and Mary were laid to rest in St. Michael's Cemetery. Their farm had been signed over to their lawyer, a Mr. Finn, to pay for their defence. Their three young daughters were put into foster care. But the case did not end with the Aylwards' burial. For months afterwards it was discussed in various newspapers. Although some editorialists downplayed the conflict between Catholic and Protestant factions, it was hard to ignore the role cultural and economic differences had played in the trial. Questions were raised about the weight given to Alexander Munro's testimony. As someone involved in the events that led to the murder charges, he was hardly a disinterested party. William Munro's refusal to press charges was also cited as strong evidence that the Munros had been the aggressors.

As for Isabella McCrea's comments that Mary Aylward had talked of killing her neighbour, there was always the possibility that Isabella had lied or exaggerated a relatively harmless conversation. If Mary, who seemed reasonably intelligent, had actually been planning to kill William Munro, would she not have kept such a plan secret?

In the end, all the analysis and speculation made absolutely no difference to Richard or Mary Aylward. They had paid the ultimate penalty for their quarrel with their neighbours. As well, Mary achieved a gruesome kind of celebrity. She was the first woman in Canada to be hanged alongside her husband.

Chapter 3
Phoebe Campbell: "You Know What I Say Is True"

T he night of July 14, 1871 was a warm one in Nissouri Township, a rural Ontario area between Woodstock and London. Through most of the evening and on into the early hours of morning, the only sounds to be heard were those of nocturnal creatures — crickets, frogs, night-hunting birds of prey. Then, on the Craig farm, hired hand Robert McDonald became aware of another sound. Somewhere in the darkness a woman was calling for help. He alerted his brother, Hugh McDonald, who woke up their employer, farmer William Craig. The two men followed the voice to George Campbell's property, where they found Campbell's 23-year-old wife, Phoebe, clinging to the fence, clad only in her petticoat. She told a horrific story

— two mysterious intruders had murdered her husband in their log cabin.

Examining the cabin by lantern light, McDonald and Craig found George's body. He had been struck several times with an axe and his throat had been cut. Blood was spattered about the cabin's single room, which was also strewn with a number of the Campbells' personal items. A pistol lay on the floor.

After they led Phoebe and her two young children to Craig's place, several neighbourhood men formed a search party and went looking for tracks that might lead them to the intruders. Phoebe later filled in the details of the story. She and George had gone to bed around eleven o'clock. Phoebe lay on the side of the bed closest to the wall, with her baby in her arms. George took the outer side of the bed, while their three-year-old daughter slept next to them in her trundle bed. Some time later, Phoebe was suddenly awakened by violent voices. According to Phoebe, two men had broken into the cabin and were threatening George. Both had blackened their faces and "talked darkey," presumably in an attempt to disguise their voices.

The couple had been living in the cabin barely a month. Married for just over four years, George and Phoebe had lived with her parents for a time, then in a temporary place of their own, before moving to the little cabin on a knoll at Lot 17, Sixth Line.

George was a farmer. Outside the Campbell cabin was

a field of wheat and another of oats. But, like many farmers of the day, he supplemented his income by cutting wood. Phoebe's father, Joseph McWain, was a contractor who supplied wood for the Grand Trunk Railway. George had recently been paid, and it seemed the intruders had robbery on their minds when they got to the Campbells' house. That was when things got out of hand. Although George tried to defend himself, he had little chance. After killing him, the intruders searched the cabin. They tossed clothing and other items about, but found nothing except a child's bank.

Phoebe repeated her story to anyone who would listen, including Detective Harry Phair of the London police force. By Sunday, the day of George's funeral, police had enough evidence to arrest one man, Thomas Davis, a farmer who lived next door to the Campbells.

It was the beginning of a bizarre series of arrests that seemed more like a fishing expedition than serious detective work.

Davis was a married man with a distinctly unsavoury reputation. According to the *London Free Press*, he had a "large flat nose, sunken eyes, and rather high cheek bones, with a comparatively low brow." At a time when many people believed in physiognomy (a pseudo-science that claimed a person's character was revealed in facial features), Davis appeared to be a likely suspect. He had a knife in his possession. And, curiously, some of his clothing had been freshly laundered. In fact, his garments were still damp when the police found them. Since laundry was almost always done on Mondays, it seemed Davis must have had a very urgent reason to wash his clothing so late in the week. Suspecting that he was trying to eliminate bloodstains, the police sent the clothes to the University of Toronto for analysis.

Three days after the funeral Detective Phair drove out to Nissouri in his buggy. He wanted to ask Phoebe several questions away from her familiar surroundings, so he drove her to London's city hall. The following day, John Barry and John McWain were taken into custody. John Barry was a 30-year-old labourer who was known to associate with a number of disreputable characters. John McWain, another resident of Nissouri Township, was Phoebe Campbell's cousin. About 40 years old and married, McWain was the father of four children and about to become the father of a fifth. He had a small 50-acre farm, but he was far from the most respectable character in the area. In fact, he was a petty thief and had been sent to jail in Stratford at least once. McWain also had the unusual habit of wandering about at night, something his neighbours viewed with suspicion. He explained it away by claiming he was near-sighted and could actually see better after dark.

On July 21, nearly a week after the murder, two more men were arrested. James Priestley was brought in for questioning mostly because, like Barry, he was known to have disreputable associates.

Thomas Coyle was another matter. As far as the McWains were concerned, Coyle was virtually a member of the family.

For the past four years he had worked as a hired man for Joseph McWain, Phoebe's father, even sleeping in a shared upstairs bedroom with three of the McWain children. But rumours in the township that Coyle and Phoebe had become a little too close after her marriage to George Campbell apparently provided enough motive, in the eyes of the police, to justify arresting him.

Attempted robbery, however, still seemed to be the strongest motive for the murder. George had frequently commented to neighbours that he had enough money to buy a farm of his own. Many people assumed that meant he kept cash at home. In fact, his capital was in the form of two promissory notes. One, for $500, was from his father in payment for work he had done on the elder Campbell's farm. The other represented wages he had earned while cutting wood.

Along with the arrests of Priestly and Coyle, July 21 brought another surprise. Phoebe Campbell and her father travelled to London to visit a lawyer, where they laid a complaint against Detective Harry Phair for "assaulting and ill-treating" her.

Then, on July 24, the day their complaint was heard before a police magistrate, Phoebe Campbell and her father, Joseph McWain, were arrested for complicity in the murder of George Campbell.

Phoebe appeared in police court dressed entirely in black. Although she seemed "a little downcast" to the *London Free Press* reporter who covered the proceedings, her colour was good and she seemed to be in generally good shape. "She is a woman of about medium height, rather stoutly formed, and appears to be in robust health." According to her version of events, when Phair picked her up in his buggy he said nothing about a subpoena or warrant for her arrest. She had no idea she was a suspect in her husband's murder.

About halfway to London, Phoebe and Phair stopped at Hueston's Tavern. "He wanted me to drink," Phoebe told the court. When Phoebe refused to enter the tavern, Phair went in on his own and brought her a glass of wine. She took a few sips and then they continued.

As they rode along, Phair asked if George had ever taken her out for buggy rides. Not very often, Phoebe replied. "Would you not like to go buggy riding with me?" the detective asked.

"No sir," Phoebe told him, and Phair replied, "I would like to go buggy riding with such a fine-looking woman as you." Phoebe paused to let the spectators who jammed the courtroom absorb her statement. Then she continued. Although she told Phair she did not want to go buggy riding with him, he put his arm around her and tried to kiss her. She pushed him away, but he persisted and asked, "if I wouldn't 'get out of the buggy with him down in the woods where no one would see us', and I told him I would not."

As Phair continued his advances Phoebe chided him, first reminding him that she was recently widowed, then warning him that she would report his behaviour. He shrugged off her threat, saying, "O, I am a gentleman, there would be no harm in that."

On the outskirts of London, Phair once again stopped at a tavern. This time Phoebe went inside, to a room where other women were gathered. Phair brought her wine but she refused to drink. Instead, she took a few sips of water and ate some cakes she had brought along in her pocket. When they reached London, Phair took her to his own house for dinner, then to City Hall. There, she told the court, he tried to kiss her while they were in one of the rooms. "He wanted me to 'cuddle' him," she reported.

At this point the police magistrate asked, "Did Mr. Phair put his hand on you in an indecent manner?"

"Yes," Phoebe replied. She also reported that, when her father came to drive her home in his wagon, she had told John McWain what happened, pointing out the various spots where Phair had made advances. The following day, they lodged their complaint.

Several witnesses testified to the detective's good character. Then Phair himself questioned Phoebe. Had it not been raining on the day in question? And had they not stopped because she seemed cold and some wine might warm her up? The proceedings ended inconclusively with the police magistrate ruling that Phoebe's credibility and the outcome of the coroner's inquest would be key elements in helping him arrive at his verdict.

The inquest began on July 25. Dozens of people

crammed into a hall attached to Garner's Hotel in Thorndale, a few miles from the scene of the murder. Witness after witness testified — about the relationship between George and Phoebe, about George's financial situation, about conflicts with the neighbours. George emerged as a hard-working, pleasant fellow, praised by most who knew him, including his father-in-law and former employer, Joseph McWain. The Campbell family, however, did not hold a similarly high opinion of Phoebe. According to John Campbell, George's father, Phoebe seldom visited the Campbell home. George's sisters were not particularly friendly with Phoebe, and John admitted he had passed by her in public without speaking to her. From the very first, he admitted, he had not thought she would fit in well with the Campbell family. When his son first introduced her, he recalled, "She appeared to me to be of a very tyrannical disposition, while he was the very reverse. She sometimes got in a violent passion with me, and you might hear her thirty or forty rods off."

Some of their disagreements seemed to be about money. Like many young men of the time, George had worked for his father without pay until he was 21. At that point he wanted to go to work for himself, but his father persuaded him to stay until the farm was free of debt. In payment he promised to give George 150 acres of his own. George stayed for another few years, accepted the property, and then decided he really wanted more independence. He asked his father for cash. Unable or unwilling to pay, John Campbell had issued a promissory note for $500, to be paid within four years. At first George seemed satisfied. But some time later he went back to his father and asked him to put a clause in his will to make sure he would be paid in the event of John's death. John Campbell implied Phoebe might have been behind this request, as she also wanted her name to appear on the promissory note.

The most dramatic evidence centred on Thomas Coyle, the hired man who worked for Phoebe's parents. A clerk from Freeman & Taylor's hardware store in St. Mary's testified that a young man who looked very much like Coyle had bought a pistol from him. He admitted he wasn't completely certain about Coyle's identity, but he confidently identified the gun found near George Campbell's body as one that had been sold around the time in question.

Testimony from Phoebe's parents confirmed that Thomas had gone into St. Mary's around the time the gun was sold. However, the McWains also provided the young farmhand's best alibi.

The McWain house was typical of many log cabins. A single main floor room was used for cooking, eating, and other tasks during the day. At night, it doubled as a bedroom. Above it, a loft served as a second bedroom. This was accessible only by a ladder connecting it to the cabin's main room. Anyone who wanted to leave or enter the loft had to pass through the main room. The two loft windows were eight or ten feet above ground level, making them too high to jump from safely or quietly. There were no buildings adjoining the cabin that might have made it possible for an agile man to leave the loft and return. And, according to witnesses, Joseph McWain did not own a spare ladder.

On the night of the murder Joseph McWain had gone to bed around eight o'clock. His three sons and Thomas went to bed about an hour later. Some time during the night Joseph wakened. It was warm and his leg was bothering him. He sat up for an hour or two with his leg propped up to ease the pain. Then he went back to bed. He swore that Thomas Coyle could not have left without waking him. His wife Mary Ann and their teenage niece, who slept in the downstairs room, offered similar testimony.

Most of the evidence presented at the inquest was circumstantial. Members of the jury had to rely heavily on their impressions of the various witnesses. The Campbells, according to newspaper reports, seemed respectable and very intelligent. The McWains were another story. Joseph McWain, it was said, had vowed to burn down his daughter's log cabin after the murder, just to stop sightseers from visiting. Resenting Detective Phair's questioning during the investigation, he had threatened him with bodily harm if he ever set foot on McWain property again. He had also backed up his daughter in her complaint against the detective. As for Phoebe's mother, Mary Ann, newspaper accounts implied she was being deliberately dramatic. "She 'took on' a good deal while telling what she knew. She appeared to be in a fainting condition, and groaned continuously." In view of numerous inconsistencies in Phoebe's version of events, it seemed the McWains' testimony could not be fully trusted.

When proceedings adjourned on July 25, three suspects — Davis, Priestley, and Barry — were released. The inquest resumed on August 4. Although the lack of conclusive evidence was still bothersome, by a process of elimination the jury concluded two people were probably responsible for the murder of George Campbell. Phoebe Campbell and Thomas Coyle were remanded in custody until the preliminary hearing. John McWain, Phoebe's cousin, was set free.

Phoebe, who was in custody in the county jail when the sheriff informed her of the verdict, at first seemed calm and unconcerned. Within a few hours, however, she decided to make a confession. She sent for Crown Attorney Charles Hutchinson, who took down her statement. This time, there was no talk of two men in blackface. She said only one man had come into the cabin. That man was Thomas Coyle. The noise made when he hit George with the axe had wakened her. When George called out for help, Phoebe had struggled out of bed and grabbed up the butcher's knife. Coyle threatened to kill her as well if she interfered, so Phoebe dropped the knife. She pleaded with Coyle, asking him why he was murdering George, and he told her that he was getting even with him for "a fuss" they had been involved in years earlier, when they had fought over the correct way to store oats. But there had been no suggestion of hostility between them since then.

Phoebe Campbell: "You Know What I Say Is True"

Coldly, Coyle told Phoebe people would suspect her of George's murder, and said she would hang. Then he threatened to kill her if she breathed a word about his identity.

As soon as she had made her statement, Phoebe asked to be allowed to visit Coyle, whose cell was on the floor below hers. Presumably some jail staff, and possibly the Crown attorney himself, witnessed their meeting, as their conversation was subsequently reported in the *London Free Press*.

"Well, Tommy," Phoebe began, "I have confessed it all."

"What have you confessed?" Coyle asked

"Why, the murder of George. I said you did it."

"You did, did you? And what did you say I did it for?"

"You know very well what it was for."

"Was it because he choked me in the mow? That was a long time ago." Sarcastically, he continued, "You're a nice woman. You've got all your relations clear and want to clear yourself and lay it on me." He paced angrily about the cell, refusing to say another word, and Phoebe turned away.

The next day, Sunday, Phoebe sent again for Crown Attorney Hutchinson. This time, she had a completely different story to tell. During the night she had experienced a vivid dream, or perhaps a vision. George had come to her and taken her by the hand. "Phoebe," he told her, "you are innocent. And that poor boy below stairs is innocent, too."

Hutchinson pointed out that she had blamed the murder on Thomas Coyle only the day before. "Well, I know I told a lie," Phoebe said, "and I am sorry for it. I hope God will

41

forgive me for what I have done." And then she revealed the "true" killer, her cousin, John McWain.

Once word had spread about Phoebe's arrest, all kinds of people called at the jail to catch a glimpse of her. The attention did not seem to bother her in the least. When someone suggested it might be less disturbing to have her photograph posted at the front of the building, she became quite excited, saying she would like to send a picture of herself to her family. Mr. Egan, a local photographer, brought his equipment into the jailhouse and took her picture on the afternoon of August 8. There was apparently a bit of discussion about what would be done with the photos. It would not be "nice," someone said to Phoebe, if Egan made additional prints from the negative and sold them as souvenirs. Phoebe shrugged off that concern, apparently less worried about Victorian niceties than about gaining a bit of fame.

By this time, Phoebe and her father had dropped their charges against Detective Harry Phair. On August 8 the detective went to John McWain's house, arriving just as he was sitting down to dinner with his wife. Phair allowed him to finish the meal, then took him into custody. Protesting his innocence and "crying like a child," McWain meekly allowed himself to be taken back to jail in London.

The preliminary hearing began on August 10. Phoebe again provided a colourful account of what had happened in her cabin on the night of July 14. In this version, she claimed that McWain, who also chopped wood to supplement his income, had used his own axe to murder George. Then he had told her to fetch George's axe, which he smeared with blood. He did the same to George's butcher knife. It was actually John McWain, Phoebe said, who had threatened to kill her if she identified him.

When asked about her cousin's motive, Phoebe had a ready answer. There was bad feeling between her cousin and her husband, she said. When her cousin John McWain was serving a sentence in the Stratford jail, he had asked George to cut firewood for his wife. George had done so, but along with cutting firewood he had gone to bed with Mrs. McWain.

McWain himself dismissed the story as ridiculous. He had cut wood with George Campbell, "and a nicer man I never knew." He had heard the rumours about George's involvement with his wife, but didn't believe George was the type of man who would do such a thing. As far as his wife was concerned, McWain added, "I courted her too long, and have been married to her too long, not to know that I can trust her." In addition, he said, a number of neighbours would testify that George had never cut wood at McWain's place while he was in Stratford jail.

In 1870s courtrooms, the accused were sometimes allowed to question their accusers directly. Now John McWain confronted his cousin.

"Phoebe, I want you to look me full in the face."

"Sir!"

"Wasn't George and I always on good terms? Come now!"

Phoebe admitted she had never heard them quarrel, but she had heard the story about McWain's wife.

"Now, Phoebe; you know you are swearing my life away, don't you?"

"No, John. For you know what I say is true."

A murmur of excitement swept over the courtroom. McWain protested that he could get witnesses that would prove that George had never cut wood on the property. But his cousin was adamant. "You know well enough you done that job; you can't deny it. You may try to deceive your fellow creatures here on earth, but you cannot deceive God!"

There was a collective gasp from the courtroom. Was Phoebe right after all? Would an accused murderess dare invoke God's name unless she had truth on her side?

But at least one person was more amused than thunderstruck, knowing that a very short time earlier, a certain woman had visited the women's section of the jail. This woman believed it was her Christian duty to bring comfort to convicted prostitutes and set them on the path of righteousness. On her last visit, within earshot of Phoebe Campbell, she had spoken those very words: "You may try to deceive your fellow creatures here on earth, but you cannot deceive God!" That small detail was duly reported in the London newspaper.

When the preliminary hearing ended, John McWain

was set free. Phoebe and Thomas Coyle remained in custody throughout the fall and winter. Except for the purchase of the pistol and Phoebe's dubious testimony, the case against Coyle was not particularly strong. Evidence against Phoebe was another matter. On April 6 she stood trial for the murder of her husband. The evidence, most of which had become common knowledge in London and the surrounding countryside, was rehashed once again. When the trial ended, Phoebe was sentenced to hang. There was no recommendation for mercy.

A few weeks later, Phoebe wrote yet another confession. This time, she claimed George Campbell had abused and mistreated her. She had been miserable, and had stated frequently that she wished she had never married. Thomas Coyle had become aware of her feelings and offered to make her single again "if she would love him." But, just as she had refused Harry Phair's advances, she refused to listen to Thomas — at first. Then the two became closer and talked about poisoning George. They went as far as obtaining poison, but Phoebe found herself unable to add the chemicals to George's food. Finally they decided they would kill him in the cabin and make it look like a robbery. A date was agreed upon: Wednesday, July 12. Phoebe was supposed to unlock the cabin door and wait for Coyle's signal, but she fell asleep. He confronted her the next day and asked if she wanted to try again. She agreed. On the night of the 14th, after George was asleep, she waited for Coyle's knock, got out of the bed and let him into the cabin. However, according to this version, Phoebe then tried to stop Coyle from murdering her husband.

As usual, Phoebe's story was full of contradictions. Her father had testified that, in all his 55 years, he had never locked the door of his home. Phoebe herself had stated that her own cabin door was seldom locked. Why, then, would she have needed to get up and unlock the door in order for Coyle to enter the cabin? Medical experts had testified that George's throat had been cut after death, while his body was lying on the cabin floor. Phoebe said the doctors were wrong — the murderer had slashed George's throat while he was still alive and standing. As well, after her sentencing she had reverted to her original story about two blackfaced men, then accused her cousin John McWain once again. Given the sheer number of accounts she had sworn to, in such varied and contradictory detail, how believable was this version?

Certain questions about Thomas Coyle were never satisfactorily answered, including the reason for his purchase of a pistol in St. Mary's. As well, Phoebe's brothers had reluctantly admitted to the prosecution that there was a slight chance the defendant might have been able to leave the loft bedroom undetected. But Coyle's defence lawyer had little difficulty persuading the jury to accept the accused as a victim of Phoebe's deadly plans. Thomas Coyle was acquitted and released.

Phoebe spent her final days singing, praying and telling everyone who would listen that she was looking forward to a better world. On Tuesday, June 18, she said goodbye to her family. The following day she bid a brief farewell to Thomas Coyle. At eight o'clock on the morning of Friday, June 20, she took her final walk. Condemned prisoners usually had their arms tied behind them, but Phoebe Campbell was unbound. In one hand she clutched an embroidered handkerchief. She walked to the gallows with a firm step and her voice was strong and vital as she accompanied a clergyman in prayer. The minister read her statement, a typical Victorian confession of guilt, complete with a warning to others not to follow in her footsteps and a wish for a better life hereafter. The hangman placed the noose around her neck, the trap door opened and Phoebe plunged through. She died instantly of a broken neck. When her body was taken down for burial in the London jail yard, the handkerchief was still in her hand.

Chapter 4
Maria McCabe:
"I Did a Bad Deed"

Maria McCabe was cold and miserable. It was March 7, 1883 — still winter in Hamilton, although there were small signs that spring would be coming soon. In Ireland, the grass would already be green.

Ah, Ireland. Maria sighed. She had been born in Ireland, the daughter of a Dublin ironmonger. Life had been hard enough for Maria, her parents, and eight brothers and sisters. It was always a struggle to find enough to eat. But fate had worse in store. In 1871, when Maria was just six years old, her mother had died. Then her father was blinded in an accident and could no longer support his family. The McCabe children were sent to a Catholic orphanage. By the time Maria entered adolescence, seven of her siblings were dead, victims of the poverty and disease that plagued so many in the cities of Ireland, Scotland, and England.

Then came a lucky break. For years, British charitable organizations, including some run by Catholic groups, thought they had a solution to the problems of the poor. There were simply not enough opportunities in Britain — not enough jobs, not enough housing, not enough clean air, nourishing food, or pure water — to keep people healthy enough to work when work was available. But opportunities existed elsewhere. Across the ocean, in British colonies such as Canada, were wide-open spaces, clean air, new towns and cities, and new businesses and industries. In Canada, anyone willing to work could live decently, perhaps even prosper. And so huge numbers of the poor, including thousands upon thousands of children, were packed into ships and sent across the Atlantic.

Maria reached Hamilton in 1880. She was 14, not quite a woman but no longer a child. She quickly learned that Canada was no paradise. There were no streets paved with gold, no easy way to earn a fortune. Certainly there was work, especially for a strong and determined girl like Maria who had already known years of arduous labour in the convent where she was raised. But few choices were available to someone with her limited education. There was needlework, if you had the skill and patience for it. In a factory you could earn good wages working alongside other young women, and your time was your own once the workday was done, but you had to pay for your own food and shelter. You'd be lucky to have any money left over once that was done.

This encouraged many immigrant women to enter domestic service in private homes, where room and board was included. Although a few wealthy households in Hamilton and elsewhere employed a large domestic staff, most families could afford just one servant. Typically a single maid-of-all-work was run ragged by her household chores, even if the mistress worked alongside her, as many still did. Most employers wanted them on call from dawn until long after dusk, day after day, begrudging even a day of rest come Sunday or a few hours to visit with friends or walk out with a handsome fellow. Hardest of all was the isolation. Often, domestic servants were terribly lonely, rarely able to socialize with people who shared their interests and background.

But there were other places where a girl could find work as a servant. Places where you still had a roof over your head and regular meals, but could get away from prying eyes and do what you pleased when your duties were done, with plenty of chances to meet people. A hotel — that was the very thing!

Maria soon found work in a Hamilton hotel.

It suited her perfectly. She made some friends, including one special young man, a businessman who visited the hotel frequently. Gradually, their friendship deepened into something more. They became lovers. Then, in the late winter of 1882, Maria became pregnant.

Maria McCabe: "I Did a Bad Deed"

She was 16, still innocent enough to think her lover would marry her, or at least help care for the baby. But when she told him her news, he just laughed. She was the one who was pregnant — it was her problem.

In desperation, Maria hid her condition as long as she could. But as her slight figure thickened, it became obvious to everyone at the hotel that she was expecting a child. There was no question of her keeping her job. A visibly pregnant single woman was an affront to every respectable person who visited the hotel. Besides, sooner or later her condition would limit her ability to perform her job.

Whatever money she had been able to put aside was quickly gone. Maria had no choice but to ask help from charitable organizations. In Hamilton, as in most Canadian cities at the time, several such organizations were in operation. Some had been created specifically to help poor immigrants, others to help needy women. A few were aimed specifically at young women like Maria, who had lost jobs or been thrown out of homes because of extra-marital sexual activities or pregnancies. Victorians typically referred to these unfortunates as "fallen women" or "Magdalenes," after Mary Magdalene, the reformed prostitute who followed Jesus.

The latter label hinted at the change of attitude that had arisen during the late nineteenth century, along with better education for women and a campaign for political equality. If Jesus could forgive a prostitute and accept her as one of his disciples, Victorians reasoned, then it was their Christian duty to do what they could to see that other women followed Mary Magdalene's example. They were more than willing to reach out to their fallen sisters, to provide them with food, shelter, medical attention, and employment. But there was a catch. Resources were limited, so the middle-class women and men who ran Magadelene organizations confined their "rescue work" to women they felt were truly deserving. That usually meant the woman not only had to be needy, she also had to be sincerely sorry for what she had done, sincerely willing to change her ways, and sincerely grateful for her rescuers' efforts.

Maria McCabe did not make the grade. She was certainly needy because, although she was willing to work, she was unable to find employment because of her pregnancy. She was probably sorry she had become pregnant, although she may still have felt some love for the father of her child. But while she might have felt some gratitude toward anyone who was willing to help her, Maria was an independent girl. She was used to looking after herself and unwilling to let anyone take advantage of her. As one of her early Hamilton employers noted, she would "brook no guff" from anyone. She might have been able to go through the motions of remorse and gratitude — but something in her face, something in her posture, revealed her true feelings. Charity after charity turned her down.

Somehow Maria survived. On November 5, 1882, she gave birth to a little boy at Hamilton General Hospital. Soon she was ready to find work, but having an infant son created a new set of problems. No one wanted to employ a woman with a child. Maria could not afford to have someone else care for her baby. She went to the child's father, asking for some financial help. Again, he refused.

Finally, someone did offer a helping hand. Ann Foster lived with her husband James at 182 Hughson Street. The couple had no children of their own and they were considering adoption. The Fosters and Maria struck a deal. If they could adopt the baby at the end of a year, Ann and James would give Maria a job until then. That way she could be close to her son and care for him until he was weaned. In addition to room and board, Ann Foster even offered Maria a small salary, one dollar per month. With no other choices available, Maria agreed.

The arrangement was far from perfect. Maria chafed at her lost independence and the close scrutiny she was under day after day in the Foster home. She and her mistress quarrelled frequently, sometimes about Maria's duties, often about the way the child should be dealt with. Sometimes, the disagreements became so heated that Ann Foster told her to leave. On at least two occasions, furious at the way she was being treated, Maria did.

After the first time, Maria and Ann managed to patch up their dispute. The second quarrel took place in early March 1883. After spending several hours walking the city streets, trying to find a job or someone who would help her and her baby, Maria was depressed and miserable. She had no choice but to swallow her pride one more time.

As she swung open the gate to the Fosters' yard, Maria thought about the changes the baby had brought to her life. The loss of her job, the disdainful comments from acquaintances and charity workers, the humiliation of having to put up with Ann Foster's demands — all could be traced to the little bundle in her arms. She would be far better off without him!

The thought had barely crossed her mind when she caught sight of an unused cistern, a large tank for storing rainwater. Impulsively, she pushed off the lid, tossed the baby in, and closed the cistern. Then she walked into the house.

Once again, Ann Foster was willing to let bygones be bygones. Maria was welcome to resume her duties. But what had happened to the baby? Maria told Ann she had found a place to board the little boy and that he would be staying there from now on. Over the next couple of weeks, Ann Foster asked directions to the baby's boarding house. Maria refused to give her any information and Ann, who had already begun to lose interest in the idea of adopting a child, gradually stopped asking questions. A short time later, Maria found work at the Victoria Hotel and left the Fosters.

Winter passed. Spring gave way to summer. As the temperature rose, Ann Foster became aware of an increasingly foul smell coming from the back yard, directly under her bedroom window. She wondered if the water in the cistern had become stagnant. Ann found her answer when she pushed open the cover and peered inside. Something was floating in the water.

At first, Ann wasn't sure what she was looking at. There seemed to be four little eggs floating on the water, with a darker form just below the surface. From time to time, small animals had been known to find their way into cisterns and drown. Ann assumed this was one of those cases. She called to her new servant, Mary McMahon, telling her that a dog or something had fallen into the cistern. Mary arrived with a pitchfork and pushed at the little body. It rolled over, and the women stared in horror as they realized they were looking at the remains of a small child.

They looked at each other, then back to the gruesome discovery, unsure what to do next. At that moment, police constable John Knox happened to be passing by. They called out to him. Knox retrieved the body and, as he did, Ann recognized the dripping garments. She had bought those clothes herself — for Maria McCabe's baby.

Constable Knox took the remains to Hamilton General Hospital and arranged for an autopsy. He then reported to the chief of police, A.D. Stewart. A short time later Stewart ordered one of his men, Constable Pinch, to go to the Victoria Hotel and bring in Maria.

There was no resistance from the young woman. Instead, she seemed relieved that her crime had finally been discovered. The result of Stewart's interview was printed in the *Hamilton Spectator* the following day:

She said she was sorry for what she had done, and was willing to suffer now for her crime, and she was glad it had been found out and the baby's body found. She said she had killed the child, because Mrs. Foster had turned her out of the house twice. She had no home and no place to go. She felt miserable and sad and saw nothing but trouble and disgrace in the future for herself and her little one.

Ann Foster corroborated Maria's description of her state of mind. More than once, she recalled, Maria had threatened to kill herself and the baby in order to escape her misery and disgrace.

Meanwhile, a coroner's jury had been empanelled. They viewed the body, then heard testimony from Dr. Leslie, the physician who had conducted the post-mortem. Decomposition made it impossible to tell the cause of death, but there was little doubt in the minds of the jury that the baby had drowned. Once the formality of the inquest was over, the baby was taken away for burial.

On August 7 Maria appeared at a preliminary hearing. The only witnesses were Chief Stewart and Dr. White, the coroner. Once their evidence was processed, Maria was sent back to jail to await trial at the fall assizes.

By this time, her story was the talk of the town. Initially, there was a feeling of horror and revulsion, plus some satisfaction that Maria had finally been caught. "She was sick of it, she said, and wanted to get rid of it," the *Hamilton Spectator* reported on August 2 when describing Maria's arrest. "She succeeded in getting rid of it. But retribution is sure to come on evil-doers and it has come to Maria."

A day later, however, with more details out in the open, a definite note of sympathy was detected in the newspaper's editorial. The brief essay pointed out that there were lessons to be learned from Maria's sad experience, and that her disgrace should be a warning to other young women. Obviously she had been a respectable person; otherwise she would not have felt so deeply ashamed of her sin. "The wonder is that she did not also make away with herself." However, the editorial continued, there were other things that ought to be considered:

> *Maria McCabe was sinned against; and what of the man through whose instrumentality she fell. There should be no half-way measures. The officers of the law should seek him out and bring him before the bar of justice; and the people of Hamilton will not be true to themselves if, when he is discovered, they do not treat him with all the scorn and contempt his cowardly conduct deserves. Society is too prone to condone the offense of the man and make the woman suffer. Justice requires that he who tempts a woman to commit a wrong should be punished as a co-partner in her guilt.*

In other articles, the *Hamilton Spectator* hinted that the man in question was well known in the city's business community. But his name was never revealed and he apparently went unpunished while Maria waited in her jail cell.

On October 16 Maria McCabe was arraigned. Two days later she went to trial before Judge Morrison. She sat in the prisoner's dock, her grey eyes swollen and red from weeping. When she spoke her voice was so low it was difficult to hear what she said.

Because Maria had pleaded guilty there was no need for a jury. Once the details of the case were entered into the record, all that remained was for Judge Morrison to pass sentence. It was 2:30 in the afternoon when he was ready to do so.

Because the acoustics in the courtroom were so bad, the judge had Maria come close to the bench. A hush fell upon the courtroom. Morrison talked quietly to Maria, tears filling his eyes as he told her how sorry he was to have to pass sentence upon her. Her case, he said, was "peculiarly pitiable and unfortunate," and he would do everything in his power to intercede with the government. And then, as the silence deepened in the courtroom, he pronounced the only punishment then permissible under Canadian law:

> *The sentence of this court on you, Maria McCabe,*
> *is that you be taken to the place from whence you*

came, and that on the 18th day of December next
you be taken to the place of execution, and be
hanged by the neck until you are dead; and may
God have mercy on your soul.

Maria burst into tears. As the slim 18-year-old was led back to her jail cell, her sobs gradually faded, but those in the courtroom still heard them in their hearts.

At an earlier time, justice was administered speedily, usually within a few days after a trial ended. By 1883 Canadian law allowed several weeks between sentencing and execution, time enough to launch an appeal and allow careful scrutiny of the case. Given the amount of interest in Maria's situation, it was a foregone conclusion that an appeal would be filed. But Hamiltonians were not taking any chances. A special session of the Grand Jury was held at which a petition was drafted, asking for clemency for Maria McCabe. Meanwhile, individual citizens and various organizations in Hamilton sent letters and petitions to the federal government.

On November 10 the Privy Council met in Ottawa to discuss the case. By the time they were finished, they had agreed the death penalty should be overturned. That afternoon a telegram was sent to the Hamilton sheriff advising him of their decision. Six days later, official notice came from Ottawa. Maria's life was spared. Instead, she was sentenced to 14 years in Kingston penitentiary.

Many of those who pleaded for clemency were outraged. Fourteen years was nearly a lifetime, especially for a girl as young as Maria. Yet when a reporter interviewed her the day after the reprieve was announced, Maria declared herself satisfied. Asked if she thought the prison sentence was too long, she replied, "No, I do not. I did a bad deed and I deserve punishment for it."

Many disagreed, especially those who believed Maria had been seriously wronged by the man who had fathered her child. As far as they were concerned, Maria had already suffered enough. More petitions and letters were sent to Ottawa. Influential Hamiltonians discussed her case whenever they could. There were promises of a home and employment for Maria as soon as she was released from prison. Finally, around the time of her twenty-fourth birthday and after nearly six years in prison, Maria was set free on May 5, 1889. She returned to Hamilton, the community that had supported her following her arrest and through the terrifying days after the death sentence was imposed.

The irony of the situation — which was probably not lost on Maria — was that some of the people who had worked so strenuously to save her from the gallows supported the same organizations that had refused to help her in the first place.

Chapter 5
Clara Ford
"Mother! Mother, I'm Shot!"

A round 10:30 on the night of October 6, 1894 Frank Westwood returned to his parents' palatial home in Toronto's Parkdale area. A few minutes after the young man went to his room, the doorbell rang. Wearing a pink shirt and a grey vest, 18-year-old Frank turned on the gaslight, crossed through the large vestibule and opened the front door about 14 inches. A shot rang out. Frank collapsed on the stairs of the vestibule while his attacker fled into the night.

Inside the house, Mrs. Westwood heard something that sounded to her like breaking glass. Then she heard Frank call out. "Mother! Mother, I'm shot!" She hurried to her son's side, followed closely by her husband. They found the vestibule full of smoke, reeking of gunpowder. Frank was on the steps, half leaning against a wall, blood flowing from a wound in the right side of his abdomen. Mr. Westwood reached for the door, but his wife pulled him back. He hurried upstairs for his own revolver, returned seconds later, then fired a shot blindly into the darkness.

The Westwoods brought their son back through the vestibule into the house then sent for medical help. Dr. A.M. Lynd soon arrived and probed the wound, but found no bullet in the abdominal cavity. He was dismayed to see no exit wound, suggesting the bullet was lodged against the young man's spine. Surgery was out of the question. It was only a matter of time before Frank would die.

In the meantime, he was still sufficiently lucid to talk with his family and the police who were called in to investigate the shooting. Frank provided a description of his assailant: a middle-aged man of medium height and slender build, wearing a dark suit and a fedora. The man had a dark complexion and a moustache. Frank claimed he did not know the shooter, although at one point he thought it might be a friend of an acquaintance. He finished his description with a cryptic comment, "Mum's the word."

Frank Westwood died at about six o'clock on the morning of October 10. His tragic death drew incredible publicity, largely because there seemed to be no motive. According to one newspaper report, "half the feminine population of Parkdale" turned out at his funeral. His murder seemed such an incredible waste. Frank was single, uninvolved with any women, "a boy of good character and reputation." By all accounts he was inoffensive and easy to get along with. Why would anyone want to shoot him?

As far as his parents were concerned, it was a case of mistaken identity. There were rumours that the murderer might have been a longshoreman Frank had caught breaking into his parents' boathouse a few weeks earlier, but that lead fizzled. Detectives continued probing.

Finally, about six weeks after the shooting, tips from police informers led them to the centre of Toronto's black community. On November 20, police officers Slemin and Porter went to a restaurant at 152 York Street. The owner, Chloe Dorsey, lived in a small upstairs apartment along with another woman, Clara Ford. The policemen said they wanted to search Clara's room. Chloe apparently was willing to co-operate, but her daughter Mamie objected. The police told Mamie to shut up or they would take her to the station.

Clara was a 33-year-old tailoress, the illegitimate daughter of a black woman and a white man. She had been on her own since the age of 12 and had a reputation as a very hard-working and industrious woman. But she was also known to go out wearing men's clothing, a practice that was not only considered scandalous by respectable Torontonians, but was also illegal. In Clara's apartment the police found men's clothing similar to that described by Frank Westwood. They also found a pistol that might have been the murder weapon. When Clara returned from work she was taken into custody and questioned by Detective Reburn and Inspector Stark. After seven hours of interrogation, she broke down and confessed. Yes, she had killed Frank Westwood. She had waited in the dark beside some bushes close to the Westwood house until she saw Frank return. Then she had rung the bell and, when he answered the door, shot him. The reason was simple: he had knocked her down and "insulted" her.

Clara's use of the word "insulted" was significant — it was a Victorian euphemism for sexual assault. When Clara accused the dead man, the police asked why she had not reported the crime. Why should she, she replied? She was a working-class, black woman. Frank was the son of a wealthy, white family. Making a complaint would have been a waste of time.

Clara's assessment was correct. Very few sexual assault charges resulted in arrests and fewer still led to a conviction. The prevailing theory was that few men would force themselves upon a virtuous woman; therefore, if a woman was attacked she must have done something to provoke the man. If the man came from a higher social class than the woman, his greater power and influence usually meant he could have any such charges dismissed or, at the very least, hire a high-priced lawyer to defend him. Besides, it was assumed that men of the upper classes were "gentlemen" who would never dream of harming any woman, especially a vulnerable working woman who probably had no male protectors.

This was the pleasant fairy tale accepted by most

respectable, middle-class Victorians. But side-by-side with this belief existed a darker story, familiar to social reformers and lovers of popular theatre. Upper-class men — gentlemen of good families, wealth and influence — *did* prey on vulnerable, virtuous women, precisely because they knew these women had little chance of bringing them to justice. That was why audiences loved melodramas where wronged heroines took the law into their own hands by killing their seducers, often disguising themselves as boys in order to get close enough to the villains.

Clara Ford seemed to fit perfectly into the mould of betrayed womanhood. Friends and co-workers described her as hard working and honest. But she was among the working poor — as a tailoress, she was somewhat more skilled than a seamstress, but her job still paid relatively low wages for which she had to work long hours. As a woman, of course, she was naturally vulnerable. And Clara was black (more specifically, "mulatto"); it was rumoured that a white man from one of the city's oldest and most respectable families had taken advantage of her mother. As a working woman and a member of what was then referred to as "the African race," Clara was close to the bottom of Toronto's social and economic ladders. Social reformers and most liberal-minded citizens believed women like Clara were deserving of pity and protection.

Toronto's blacks made up about one percent of the city's population in 1894. Most worked in menial, low-paying jobs. Many white Torontonians had never actually encountered a black individual, although they were familiar with the racial stereotypes portrayed in plays, minstrel shows, and the popular press. The most pervasive stereotypes represented black people as mentally inferior, childlike in nature, and unable to control their passions. If, as Clara claimed, Frank Westwood had "insulted" her, common wisdom held it was hardly surprising that she had retaliated by shooting him.

Clara's lawyer, E.F.B. Johnston, counted on these stereotypes as he prepared his defence. But he also had to find some way of presenting the most controversial evidence in a more positive light.

The main problems centred on Clara's sexuality. At 33, compared to Frank Westwood's 18, she could hardly play the role of innocent maiden. In addition, there was some indication that she had been married in her late teens or early twenties, although she had apparently been single for at least ten years. There was also the matter of Florence McKay, a young teenager who was rumoured to be Clara's illegitimate daughter.

Then there was Clara's habit of dressing in male clothing. According to one report, she had first dressed as a man out of necessity, while working in a livery stable. She found the attire so comfortable that she continued the practice. She was not the only woman who did so. At one point when Clara was being questioned, Inspector Stark asked her why she wore men's clothes when it was against the law. Clara snapped that another woman, Vie Steinberg, wore men's clothing to baseball and football games, as well as to the opera house, "and nothing is said about it." For some women, male attire translated to freedom, and possibly a degree of safety while out on the streets. In Clara's case, her cross-dressing fuelled all kinds of wild speculation. According to one report, she liked to eat raw meat. Another said she had spent some time as an Anglican choirboy in Chicago. Yet another said she was fast and agile enough to leap onto a Toronto streetcar when it was in motion.

Whether or not these speculations were true, none of the stories helped Johnston present Clara as a respectable woman abused by a young man of good family who should have known better. Johnston decided his best chance lay in convincing the jurors that she had been coerced into making a false confession. By the time the trial opened on April 30, 1895, he had positioned himself as a chivalrous defender of a woman wronged — but wronged by the detectives, not by Frank Westwood. To further strengthen his position, he made it known that he would work *pro bono*, charging Clara not one cent for her defence.

Facing Johnston in the courtroom was Crown Attorney Britton Bath Osler. Like Johnston, he was a highly respected lawyer. As prosecutor, he was in the awkward position of having to persuade the jury to convict a vulnerable, misguided woman who claimed to have been defending her virtue in the only way she thought possible. Unless he managed the case carefully, Osler might appear as a bully.

Fortunately, Osler's personal circumstances worked in his favour. Everyone in the courtroom could see the scars on one side of his face. It was common knowledge that he had been badly burned rescuing his wife from a house fire that had left Mrs. Osler a permanent invalid, and that he was deeply devoted to his wife. Surely no man who was capable of making such sacrifices for one woman would act callously toward another.

Clara was escorted into the courtroom by two constables. She wore a dark coat, trimmed with fur, a black dress with a prim white collar, and a black hat. She seemed very calm, "stolid, indifferent and almost uninterested," according to one newspaper. As the jurors were called one by one, she assessed them coolly, her hands folded neatly in front of her.

Over the next few days the prosecution called a total of 33 witnesses. Aside from medical testimony and ballistics evidence that matched Clara's pistol to the weapon that had killed Frank, most of the witnesses were asked questions designed to either build up Frank's character or tear down Clara's. According to Osler, Clara was not a woman wronged, but a woman scorned. As a gentleman, the Crown Attorney had no choice but to criticize Westwood "for dallying with a woman so evidently beneath him." However, in the end the young man had done the right thing by disentangling himself from the inappropriate relationship. Tragically, he had paid for this action with his life.

One of Osler's strategies was to present Clara as a

woman with a bad temper who would not accept rejection, and who thought nothing of resorting to violence. When Osler's ailing wife died midway through the trial, assistant Hartley Dewart took over the prosecution and continued that strategy. Among the people he questioned was Clara's employer, Simon Barnett, who told the court that she was a good woman, a hard worker who "didn't want to be bothered by any one when she was at work." When Dewart asked if she had a "high temper," Barnett responded, "She got a high temper, there's no use talkin'; we all got tempers, ain't we? I got as much as she has."

Chloe Dorsey, Clara's landlady, made a similar point. When Dewart asked, "Is Clara hot-tempered?" Chloe replied, "Not more so than you."

"Did you ever see me hot?"

"You're getting hot now," Chloe pointed out.

"Listen, Mrs. Crozier ..." Dewart had confused Chloe with another witness, one less friendly to Clara.

"Mrs. Crozier!" Mrs. Dorsey said indignantly, "Don't call me that name!"

Benjamin Vise, one of Clara's former employers, also characterized Clara as a hard worker. But his testimony made her seem extremely dangerous. According to Vise, one day when Clara was at work a pistol fell out of her jacket. Some of the other girls were frightened and Clara explained she would not walk anywhere without it. Vise also said that Clara had once told him she might be getting married, to a white man by the name of Gus Clarke. Vise knew him and asked, "Will Gus marry a coloured girl?" Clara replied by telling Vise that he had better. They had been out buggy-riding several nights in a row, and if he didn't marry her, she said, "I'll do him up, as I did a man in the States."

In the witness box, Clara appeared thoroughly amused by the statement. But a former co-worker, Mrs. Gussie Cohen, said Clara had also threatened to "do up" another female co-worker if she assaulted her, and another witness claimed Clara swore she would shoot Frank if she found him with another woman.

The pistol was an important part of the prosecution's case. Clara claimed she had purchased it secondhand about three years earlier, for her own protection. She had used it once, on a visit to the Toronto lakeshore the previous summer, when she had shot at two ducks, in "a spirit of devilment more than anything else." The remaining four bullets, the only bullets she had ever purchased, were still in the gun. Considerable time was spent explaining the similarities between the markings on the bullet that had killed Frank Westwood and those on bullets fired from Clara's pistol. However, although there was growing understanding of ballistic evidence, the information was not considered absolutely conclusive.

The timing of events was also questionable. Frank had been shot at 10:30. When detectives walked the most likely route between the Westwood house and Clara's apartment it took them an hour and 55 minutes to cover the distance, which meant that if Clara had shot Frank, she would have reached York Street at 12:25. Mamie Dorsey swore that on the night of the murder the door to their apartment had been locked at midnight, as it always was. The best rebuttal the prosecution could offer was that Mamie or Chloe had got the time wrong or, as the detectives suggested, Clara had been in a greater hurry than they were and so had reached her apartment more quickly.

Ultimately, the trial rested on Clara's testimony about what had happened during her interrogation. She claimed that they had not warned her that any information she gave might incriminate her. It was only when they started questioning her about the pistol that she realized they were investigating the Westwood murder. Clara was an avid newspaper reader, and the story had received wide coverage.

Initially, Clara had provided an alibi. On the night of the murder, she had visited a friend near Spadina and Adelaide Streets. Then, accompanied by Florence McKay, she had gone to the Toronto Opera House to watch a popular melodrama, "The Black Thief." She had left her apartment between seven and eight o'clock and returned a little after eleven o'clock. Furthermore, she claimed, she did not even know Frank Westwood.

It was the detectives who forced her to confess, Clara said. They kept badgering her, saying her alibi was a fabrication. All she needed to do was say that Frank had "insulted" her, they'd told her. No jury would find her guilty, especially since Frank was dead and could not deny a thing she said. In addition, one of the policemen told her with a wink, she might even be able to collect the reward that was offered for information on the case, something in the area of $500. The police would do everything they could to help her, they said. In fact, Sergeant Reburn told her "if she was his own sister he couldn't think more of her."

As the evening wore on, the detectives lost patience. "Clara, the more you deny it the worse it will be for you," Reburn threatened. Finally, at around eleven o'clock, he said, "Clara, it's getting late; I can't bother with you no more tonight; if you were a man I'd not bother with you; I'd put you downstairs. Clara, you got in a net and you can't get out of it." At that point, said Clara, she'd confessed to everything.

Earlier, Florence McKay had sworn that she had not gone to the opera house with Clara on the night of the murder. Confronted with this testimony, Clara said Florence was lying and implied that the police had pressured Florence, just as they had pressured her. Hartley Dewart cross-examined Clara for three hours, but could not get her to change her testimony. There was little sign of her now-famous hot temper, but she was adamant. The detectives had forced her into making a false confession.

The prosecution stressed that it was a standard ploy for criminals to accuse the police of wrongdoing. E.F.B. Johnston, Clara's lawyer, countered that such accusations were sometimes justified. The detectives were trying to advance their own careers by pinning the crime on a helpless woman. Their behaviour was so dishonourable, retorted Johnston, that it made him "ashamed to be a man."

In his closing arguments, Hartley Dewart relied heavily on racist and sexist sentiments. Clara, he said, was a "man-woman," unnatural and untrustworthy. Dewart compared her to "a Mexican bandit who, reckless of his own life, risked it in the robbery that added booty to his purse; and her demeanour during her trial was like that of an Indian stoic." His meaning was clear to everyone in the courtroom: like Mexicans and Native peoples, members of "the African race" were half-savage, not fully human. Dewart also pointed out a glaring contradiction between Clara's behaviour and her testimony. She claimed the detectives had worn her down with repeated questioning. But she had shown little sign of stress during the five days of her trial, even during lengthy cross-examination.

It was Johnston, however, who held the trump card. One of the difficulties facing the jury was that if they convicted Clara they were also condemning poor, dead Frank Westwood for immoral and ungentlemanly behaviour. By acquitting Clara, they could restore Frank's reputation as the affable, innocent young man his parents and friends remembered. "Think of the terrible responsibility if you make a mistake on the evidence," Johnston urged. "Think of this poor lone negro girl. Weigh the evidence and render your verdict accordingly."

The jury retired. Everyone else remained in the court-room — Clara, Frank Westwood's father, and the lawyers, witnesses, and spectators. The clock ticked off the minutes. Finally, after about an hour's deliberation, the jury returned. When the judge asked for the verdict, the foreman delivered it clearly: "Not Guilty."

Frank's father let out a long sigh as the spectators applauded. When order had been restored, the judge instructed Clara to stand. "The jury has acquitted you of the crime with which you were charged," he began. "I am not surprised at the result, and for your sake I am glad. I am not sorry at the verdict, as it has cleared your character and also the character of the poor young fellow who is dead. Let me say one word more: Be kind to the little girl, Florence McKay, who has shown her love for you, though she was compelled to testify against you. I ask you to be kind to her. Treat her gently and lovingly. You are free."

As Clara stepped down from the prisoner's dock, dozens of spectators pushed forward to shake her hand. One of her friends managed to get close and the two women embraced. Then Clara headed for Dorsey's restaurant, followed by a throng of well-wishers. Many of them pushed their way into the establishment. Police tried to maintain some semblance of order but found the task next to impossible. Finally, Chloe Dorsey barred the doors of the restaurant.

In the midst of the noisy celebration there were calls for a speech from Clara. Her words were brief. "I thank you for the way you stood by me. This does the boys of Toronto credit."

Chapter 6
Angelina Napolitano: "I Am Not a Bad Woman"

On April 16, 1911 — Easter Sunday — Angelina Napolitano killed her husband Pietro with an axe as he lay sleeping in the bedroom of their home in Sault Ste. Marie's Italian district. She calmly returned the axe to the shed, picked up her youngest son and, sitting before the fireplace in the front room, held him for about an hour. Then she went next door to her neighbour, Teodore Mazzo, told him what she had done and asked the old man to get the police.

It wasn't long before they arrived. Angelina met them at the door. "Here I am," she said. "Take me. I am ready to die."

Angelina went on trial for murder on May 8 and 9. Already parts of her story had been splashed across the pages of far-from-sympathetic local newspapers. The general consensus seemed to be that such violence was to be expected among immigrants, especially within the Italian community. In the early 1900s, when the dominant culture in Canada was white, Anglo-Saxon, and Protestant, many people believed in eugenics and social Darwinism, shaky theories that were said to prove the innate superiority of the so-called Nordic races — the British, Germans, Dutch, and Scandinavians. Those from the Ukraine, Poland, and other eastern European countries were considered less evolved, both mentally and emotionally. And people from southern Europe, whose complexions tended to be darker, were considered more inferior still. Newspapers, social agencies, the legal system, and other institutions used these beliefs to explain violence among immigrant groups, as well as to keep individuals out of well-paying and powerful positions.

The Napolitanos were part of a large wave of Italian immigrants that arrived in Canada between 1900 and 1914. Thousands pulled up their Mediterranean roots and transplanted them in the New World, hoping to earn money they could send back home to support the family farms. Angelina and Pietro were from a small town near Naples, in southern Italy. In 1898, when Angelina was 15, they married there and spent the next three years on her mother's farm. In 1901 the couple sailed for North America.

The Napolitanos' first destination was New York, then one of the biggest magnets for Italian immigrants. However, like many others, they found life in the big city difficult. They decided to move north to Canada, settling first in the pulp-and-paper town of Thessalon, Ontario, where they bought a house. But growing debts made it impossible for them to keep up their payments. By 1908 the Napolitanos and their four children had moved to Sault Ste. Marie.

In "the Soo" (as it was known) a number of industries, including the steel mill and local mining operations, were willing to hire Italian immigrants. But competition for jobs was sometimes fierce, and the majority of job seekers were single men who could live more cheaply than those supporting a household. Pietro sometimes found himself out of work. The family's financial difficulties, the loss of their Thessalon home, and a certain degree of homesickness took their toll. Pietro began to drink heavily, and abused his wife both mentally and physically.

The Napolitanos argued most frequently about money. Specifically they were at loggerheads about how Angelina could supplement Pietro's income and bring in enough extra money to allow them to build a house. Few job opportunities existed for married immigrant women in the town. Angelina's poor English, which she had little opportunity to improve, added to the difficulties. She sometimes took in boarders, but that did not bring in enough to make a significant difference.

Pietro thought he had the perfect solution — prostitution. Three-quarters of the Italian men in Sault Ste. Marie had no women with them; Angelina could make a small fortune catering to their sexual needs. Frequently, as he left for work, Pietro would say to his wife, "Now, you invite some men in here and get some money for me." When he returned to find that Angelina had refused to sell herself, he would threaten to kill her.

In mid-November 1910, Pietro was unemployed. Angelina still refused to give in to his demands so he went to Toronto looking for work. Left behind, with no money and no source of income, Angelina took in a man named Nish as a boarder. By the time Pietro returned a week later, his wife and Nish had become intimate.

Pietro completely misread the situation. He thought Angelina had finally done what he'd been urging her to do all along. Instead of becoming furious, he congratulated her.

He then made arrangements to live elsewhere, planning to come around every night and collect the money he believed Angelina was earning. But, as he soon found out, she had nothing for him. Pietro was enraged to discover that his wife had not actually prostituted herself. Defensively, she explained to Pietro that she had accepted Nish as a boarder — because she needed money to buy food for her children — and that their relationship had simply slipped out of control. Not surprisingly, as soon as Nish learned Angelina's husband was back in town, the boarder vanished.

On the third night after Pietro's return to Sault Ste. Marie, he again went to his wife asking for money. Again, Angelina told him she had none for him. More importantly, she screamed, she did not want to be married to him any longer.

Their argument escalated. Losing all control, Pietro pulled a knife from his pocket and stabbed Angelina nine times, wounding her in the chest, face, arms, and shoulder.

Their violent shouting and screaming caught the attention of neighbours, who called the police. By the time the authorities arrived to arrest Pietro, Angelina had disappeared. A police officer found her a short time later, bleeding profusely as she staggered toward the town's canal, apparently planning to kill herself. She was taken to hospital, where she spent three weeks before she was well enough to go home. Scars from the attack were still clearly visible six months later.

Pietro was charged with wounding with intent to maim. This crime, emphasized Crown Prosecutor Uriah McFadden, was a serious one. But Judge Johnson decided Pietro had been seriously provoked by Angelina's liaison with Nish. Considerable support existed within the Italian immigrant community for Johnson's decision. After hearing a report from a Children's Aid Society representative, the judge ruled it would be in the family's best interest to release Pietro on probation. That way, the judge commented, Pietro could continue to support the family, and the four children would not have to be placed in foster care. Underlying Johnson's ruling was a stereotypical picture of Italians as hot-blooded, violent individuals. And, as a *Sault Star* reporter would write later, "It was the custom in Italy to carry knives and do your own avenging."

After his brush with the law, Pietro was careful not to

physically abuse Angelina, knowing that if he used his fists or a knife on her he would undoubtedly go to jail. Besides, she was pregnant again, although it was not clear whether Pietro or Nish was the father. His emotional abuse of her, however, was unrelenting. Despite Angelina's knife scars and her pregnancy, Pietro continued pressuring his wife to sell her body. From time to time he even sent men to the house while he was at work. Although she never opened her door to them, Angelina's resolve was beginning to wear down under Pietro's constant harassment. By Easter, six months pregnant, physically scarred, and emotionally exhausted, Angelina was convinced it was only a matter of time before she would give in to her husband's incessant demands. Killing him, she concluded, was the only way out of her dilemma.

Angelina went to trial determined to plead guilty. But Justice F.M. Britton would not allow her to enter the plea, especially after he learned she had no legal representation. He appointed as her defence attorney Uriah McFadden, the same young lawyer who had prosecuted Pietro after the stabbing. McFadden hastily put together a defence, but had no time to find friendly witnesses. By noon the next day, nine witnesses had testified for the Crown.

The best McFadden could do was allow Angelina to tell her own story, through an interpreter.

"I am not a bad woman," the small, soft-spoken mother of four insisted, after revealing the details of her horrific marriage.

The court's opinion was considerably different. Angelina's affair with Nish destroyed any hope she might have held of convincing the judge and jurors she was a virtuous wife and mother, seriously wronged by a vicious and immoral husband. As far as Justice Britton was concerned, Pietro's November attack of Angelina was irrelevant, therefore inadmissible. Although McFadden tried to introduce the stabbing as evidence of the abuse that had led Angelina to murder, Britton overruled his attempts. Pietro had been asleep and utterly defenceless when his wife smashed the axe into his head. There was no possible way a beating that had happened months earlier could be interpreted as provocation, he ruled; to do so would undermine the law to the point where chaos would be the inevitable result.

Strictly speaking, Justice Britton was interpreting the law correctly, if somewhat narrowly. Courts did not yet recognize battered wife syndrome, and his only choice was to inform the jury that Angelina had no legal justification for killing her husband.

Britton also clarified the issue of Angelina's pregnancy. Should the jury find her guilty, he told them, their decision would not lead to harm for the unborn child. In accordance with longstanding legal tradition, Angelina's execution would be postponed until she had given birth.

The verdict was predictable. Angelina Napolitano was found guilty of murder. Although the jury recommended mercy, none was forthcoming. Justice Britton sentenced

Angelina to hang. He set August 9 as the date.

It was then that a howl of protest arose — not from Angelina or the local Italian community, but from feminists, civil libertarians, and Italians around the world.

According to one version of events, an American journalist who happened to be visiting Sault Ste. Marie around the time of the trial picked up the story and published it in the United States. Angelina's situation quickly became a *cause célèbre*. She was portrayed as a devoted mother with limited social and financial resources who ended an unbearable marriage in the only way she knew how. According to the popular press, she was an innocent victim. Male chauvinism had allowed Pietro to go unpunished for his abuse and psychological torture. And a combination of male chauvinism and ethnic prejudice had led to Angelina's conviction in a court of law dominated by white, Anglo-Saxon men. Had a woman of British ancestry faced the same charges, protestors argued, she would have gone free.

Italians across North America, in Toronto and Montreal, New York and Chicago, signed petitions asking for Angelina's immediate release. Meanwhile, feminists in Canada, the United States, Britain, Poland, Hungary, and Austria added their support. As American newspapers printed scathing articles about the shortcomings of a Canadian legal system that had sentenced a maltreated mother of four to death, supporters signed hundreds of petitions in Angelina's favour. By early July, according to Canadian government estimates, petitions bearing more than 100,000 signatures had been forwarded to Ottawa.

Many of the petitioners wanted Angelina's conviction overturned. Others favoured a more moderate solution. The National Council of Women, whose membership was predominantly middle-class, Anglo-Saxon, and conservative, asked only that the death sentence be commuted to life imprisonment.

Meanwhile, one of the National Council's member organizations, the Toronto Local Council of Women, lobbied to prevent the separation of Angelina's two sons and two daughters, who were all under 13 at the time of the murder. Representatives appealed to J.J. Kelso, a former journalist and superintendent of the Children's Aid Society, but their efforts ultimately failed. The children went to different foster homes around the province.

The public clamour to free Angelina, or at least ensure her survival, resulted in the largest and most controversial petitioning campaign in Canadian history up to that point. However, not everyone supported the petitioners. A.B. Aylesworth, the federal justice minister, was personally unsympathetic, labelling Angelina as "a murderer who admittedly chopped the head of a man to pieces while he was asleep." Canadians all over North America wrote to newspapers, stating their support of the death sentence. According to the *Sault Star*, no one in the town's Italian community had signed any of the petitions.

The newspaper also printed a number of rumours disguised as stories that had been circulating since the time of the murder. According to one, Angelina had been seen carefully sharpening the axe in the days leading up to Easter. According to another, she was such an unfit mother that the Children's Aid Society had threatened to take away her family prior to the November stabbing; only Pietro's intervention had stopped them.

Angelina's lawyer, Uriah McFadden, made an effort to correct the newspaper's errors. The Children's Aid Society had not been involved until they reported on the impact Pietro's incarceration would have on the family. As for the statement, "The woman actually sharpened the axe and put it carefully away in preparation of the deed," McFadden wrote, "This is where your reporter draws on his imagination." The *Sault Star* would not back down, rebutting McFadden's correction with the comment that Angelina's statement was relayed to the newspaper "by a legal gentleman very closely identified with the case. It will thus be seen that as far as the *Star* is concerned there was no 'manifest misrepresentation.'"

The *Sault Star* claimed to reflect the general consensus of the town's residents. "Mrs. Neapolitano is not the angel the American press made her out to be," the *Star* editorialized on July 6, 1911. "Of course, a worthless woman could hardly be made interesting. So Mrs. Neapolitano is painted as beauty in distress, a virtuous woman who was driven to murder to save herself from becoming a white slave." Yet, even as the words went to press, it was evident that the petitions and accompanying publicity had done their job. On July 15, 1911, Angelina's death sentence was commuted to life in prison.

She stayed in Sault Ste. Marie until her baby was born, then was sent to Kingston penitentiary. Several weeks later, the baby died. Over the next months, a number of petitions demanded her immediate release. Individuals and organizations such as the Salvation Army offered her a place to stay and financial support as soon as she was paroled. But it was more than 11 years before Angelina's parole came through on December 22, 1922.

She spent the next two years in Kingston, having been told she could not leave the city. When she discovered there were no restrictions to her movements, she left, probably heading back to Sault Ste. Marie in an attempt to find her children. Angelina Napolitano was never heard of again.

Chapter 7
Carrie Davis:
"You Have Ruined My Life"

A round six o'clock on the evening of Monday, February 8, 1915, Toronto newsboy Ernest Pelletier was making his rounds. One of his stops was at 169 Walmer Road, the luxurious home of Charles Albert (Bert) Massey, a grandson of Hart Massey, the famous agricultural equipment manufacturer. The newsboy gave a jaunty knock and the Masseys' maid, a slight, fair-haired English girl in her late teens, answered the door. When Ernest asked for payment she told him Mr. Massey was not at home, and asked him to call again.

Glancing up the street, Ernest spotted a man headed toward the house. He looked familiar. Was that Massey, he asked the maid? Yes, she told him. So Ernest began walking up the snowy street toward him. When they met, Massey paid the newsboy his money. Ernest continued along his route, while Massey made for home.

Suddenly, Ernest heard a curious popping noise. At first he thought it was an electric light bulb breaking, as they sometimes did when turned on. He turned in the direction of the sound and saw Bert Massey staggering backwards off his front porch. "Oh! Oh!" the man cried. Ernest caught a glimpse of an extended arm, a flashing pistol, and a flutter of white apron as a second shot spat out and the door was slammed shut. Bert Massey collapsed in his snowy front yard.

Several people who were on the street at the time hurried to the fallen man. One of them rang the Masseys' front doorbell, but no one responded. Massey was carried into the house next door, at 171 Walmer, and examined by Dr. John Mitchell, who also lived on the street. There was nothing the physician could do. Charles Albert Massey was dead at the age of 34.

The police arrived soon afterward. Massey's body was sent to the morgue while patrol sergeant Lawrence Brown and other officers went to his house. They rang the bell, and knocked at both front and back doors. Again, no one responded. So Brown entered, after first taking the precaution of stationing policemen at both entrances.

In the basement they found Charlie, Massey's 14-year-old son. A mechanically gifted youngster, Charlie was always tinkering and experimenting. He had been trying his hand at glass blowing, and had heard a bit of noise but had ignored it. A search of the ground floor turned up nothing. As Brown made his way to the second floor, he heard the sound of movement in the third-floor attic. He called out, "Come down. You had better surrender."

A girl's voice replied, "Come up." They met on the landing. Carrie Davis, the Masseys' maid, was wearing her coat, apparently ready to go out. In one hand she held a .32 calibre pistol, with the handle extended toward Brown. He took the gun from her, and then began asking questions. Why had she shot Massey?

"Because he ruined my life."

"Is that so?"

"Yes," Carrie told the police officer. "He ruined my character." Then she asked Brown to take her away.

When Brown first encountered Carrie, she appeared calm and was dry-eyed. But she soon broke down, sobbing, as she told her story. She was 18, and originally from Bedford, England. Her father was a disabled British army veteran who had served in the South African War, where he had suffered a leg wound that made it difficult for him to support his family. Her mother helped out by taking in sewing. When Carrie was 16 she had borrowed money from a married sister in Toronto to pay her passage to Canada. Shortly after her arrival in May 1913, she went to work as a servant in the Massey home. Her work was so satisfactory that Carrie's salary was gradually increased, so she was able to pay back her sister as well as send money home. This helped the family enormously, especially after her father died and her mother, diagnosed with cataracts, was forced to stop bringing in sewing.

Bert Massey and his wife, Rhoda, treated Carrie well. She was given regular days off and encouraged to visit the local YWCA, attend services at the Anglican Church, or spend time with family and friends. One of her closest friends was Mary Rooney, another young servant, who worked for Massey's brother.

Like many young domestics, Carrie cooked, cleaned, made beds, and carried out a number of household chores. Although the work was sometimes hard and the hours long, she seemed generally content. Then, during the first weekend of February 1915, her comfortable little world fell apart.

Rhoda Massey, Bert's wife, was an American citizen. In early February she made a visit to the United States, and Carrie promised to stay home and look after the Massey menfolk while Rhoda was away, postponing her days off until her mistress returned.

On Friday, February 5, Bert hosted a dinner party at his house. The Masseys were Methodists, a religious denomination noted for its straight-laced approach to life. Drinking, dancing, and gambling were all frowned up. Although their standards were not as restrictive as they had been in the days of Bert's grandfather, Hart Massey, the extended family still retained enough of its Methodist character to set it apart from upper-crust Toronto society. Except for Bert. According to *The Globe*, Bert was "well known about town"— a popular young man who liked sailing, fast cars, and the good life.

Twelve people attended the dinner party at the Massey house on February 5. Carrie prepared the meal and served it. There was nothing remarkable in that but, as she later testified, Massey and his guests were drinking heavily. The party broke up about midnight, with the guests giving three cheers for their host as they left the house.

Saturday was quiet, as was Sunday morning. Around 1:30 in the afternoon, Bert came downstairs in this bathrobe. By this time his son Charlie was dressed, and soon afterwards the boy went out for dinner. Massey called Carrie into the kitchen from the dining room. "Carrie, I must thank you for what you did on Friday." Then he gave her a ring — a small shamrock decorated with pearls. Massey wandered off for a bit, then came back and resumed the conversation.

"He asked me if I noticed anything Friday night. Did I see a lady drop her table napkin so many times, and did I see him run his hand up and down the lady's stocking. I didn't answer him, but just looked hard at him."

Massey was silent for a few moments, and then told her that he had a lady friend. There was some other conversation, although Carrie could not recall the details. But she did remember Massey asking her not to tell Mary Rooney or his sister.

Then he put his hands around Carrie's waist and told her he liked little girls. "He kissed me and I struggled, but he kissed me again." According to Carrie, Massey was "trembling and excited." She managed to pull away and went into the kitchen. Her employer went upstairs to his room and took a bath.

Shortly afterwards Carrie climbed the stairs, assuming Massey was still in the bath. Instead, he was in the bedroom, looking through his wife's dresser drawers. He grabbed Carrie again, talking to her as he pulled out various items of his wife's underwear. "He wanted me to put them on for him, and he came towards me and tried to throw me on the bed. I struggled and ran away from him."

Carrie ran to her own room and locked the door. There she waited for some time. Then, although it was not her scheduled afternoon off, and despite her promise to Rhoda Massey, she put on her coat and hat, tiptoed down the stairs, and went to visit her sister on Morley Avenue.

Carrie's sister was six years older and had a young family of her own. Carrie began to tell her sister what had happened, but as she described how Bert Massey had kissed her, her sister told her to be quiet. Carrie's young nephew was in the room and his mother did not want the boy to hear. Then Carrie became involved in playing with the children and no other chance arose to talk to her sister privately.

Still, she was sufficiently upset to talk to her brother-in-law, Edmond F. Fairchild. She told him about the kisses and the ring. Perhaps Bert Massey was drunk, she suggested, although he did not look that way and he was not usually a heavy drinker. Carrie said nothing, however, about the encounter in the bedroom, uncomfortable discussing the details with a man. But she did ask for Fairchild's advice. Her brother-in-law advised her to return, so she could keep her promise to Mrs. Massey. But he also told her if that if Massey made any further advances she should leave the house.

Carrie went back to Walmer Road. When she arrived, the outside lights were shining, as they usually were when the family was away. Without seeing Massey or Charlie, she went upstairs to her room.

Next morning, she called Massey at 8:45 and put his breakfast on the table. Then she went to the cellar, determined to avoid him. "I was frightened of him," she recalled. After 10 or 15 minutes she heard the front door open. Through the cellar window she watched him walk down the street.

Carrie tried to follow her usual routine — cleaning the house, cooking Charlie's lunch, and serving it to him when he came home at noon. But she could not forget the events of Sunday. "I was unable to do all my work. I kept thinking of what had happened the day before. He was my master and he kissed me and that worried me." After nearly two years in the household, she thought she knew Massey's character, and that knowledge made her deeply uneasy. "He was a man who meant to do what he said."

There was no one to whom Carrie could turn. Her brother-in-law had sent her home. Mary Rooney, the one friend she could trust, worked for Bert Massey's brother. Mrs. Massey was unreachable. Charlie was too young to rely upon. When she saw Bert Massey coming down the street at the end of the day, Carrie panicked. "I lost control of myself, and I thought of what he was going to do, and it frightened me. Everything was misty before me. I could only think of him doing me harm ... and I knew that I would have to defend myself some way or other."

She grabbed the pistol, which usually hung on the wall in Charlie's room. The boy sometimes used it for target practice in the basement and had shown Carrie how to load it. She put five bullets in the barrel, and then went to the door. Bert put his key in the lock and as the door swung open she confronted him. "You have ruined my life!" she cried as she fired the first shot. Then she shot again. Someone called out, "Stop it!" and she ran to her room, convinced she had not hit Massey.

* * *

Rhoda Massey was so overwhelmed by the shock of her husband's death that she took to bed. When a reporter from the *Toronto Evening Telegram* called to speak to Rhoda, Mrs. A.L. Massey, her sister-in-law, handled the interview. She quickly dismissed Carrie's accusation as groundless. "I know that it has been hinted that Mr. Massey may have been indiscreet and acted improperly toward the girl, but the whole story is ridiculous. No person who knew Bert will believe that for a minute. He was not the kind of man to act that way."

The problem, said Mrs. Massey, was the girl herself. She recounted an incident that had taken place the previous year at their summer home on Centre Island, across the bay from Toronto. Bert and Rhoda had come for a visit, bringing Carrie along with them. While their employers were at the yacht club, Carrie and Mary Rooney had gone to the park. Carrie suddenly became ill. When Mrs. Massey returned from the club, "she was attempting to tear her hair and bite her fingers. It took six people to hold her." Two doctors and a trained nurse were sent for and she was given the very best care.

According to Mrs. Massey, the doctors said Carrie had suffered some kind of spell. She could not be more specific, but she made it clear that there had been other signs of mental unbalance. There was no question of misbehaviour or immorality, Mrs. Massey stressed, before adding, "Once or twice I was struck by a peculiar look which she seemed to have but I put it down to her English ways and the fact that she had only been in the country two years." In addition, a seamstress who worked for her and also knew Carrie said she would not socialize with her "as there seemed to be something wrong with her mentally."

As far as the Masseys were concerned, Bert's sister-in-law continued, "There was absolutely no motive for the shooting, except that the girl was out of her head. We are sure that the shooting was due to the girl not being mentally responsible." To prove their point, they hired Dr. Beemer from the Mimico mental asylum to examine Carrie. If he declared she was mentally incompetent there would be no trial. Instead, the young servant would be confined to a mental hospital.

Some of the local newspapers, including *The Star*, took the family's statements at face value. Carrie had been carrying a heavy burden: her father's recent death, her mother's deteriorating vision, separation from most of her family, and her soldier boyfriend's posting overseas all weighed on her. World War I had been raging for eight months, and although Carrie's sweetheart was still in Salisbury, England, it was only a matter of time before he would be sent to the front. With so much to worry about, it was hardly surprising that the frail-looking young woman had lost her mind.

But had she? Dr. Beemer thought not. His diagnosis confirmed what many cynical Torontonians had already suspected. The discussion of mental illness was a strategy designed to circumvent a trial and keep Bert Massey's reputation intact.

Fortunately, Carrie had many supporters in the city — almost too many, in fact. One such advocate group was the Toronto Local Council of Women. Members were mostly from the upper middle-class, many of them social reformers dedicated to the campaign for women's rights. One of their many interests was ensuring that women, especially poor, working-class women, were treated fairly by the justice system. When the details of Carrie's case became known, they offered to provide a lawyer for her.

Meanwhile, the Bedfordshire Fraternal Association

(BFA) was also prepared to offer assistance. The BFA membership, which included Carrie's brother-in-law, consisted of working-class Englishman from her home shire who pooled money to help their own in time of sudden illness, accident, or death. Although there was some initial confusion about the duplication of efforts, the BFA soon made it clear to the Local Council of Women that they would look out for Carrie. They began a fund-raising campaign, collecting money from anyone who cared to donate. Within a few weeks the group had raised over $550, mostly from small donations of 50 cents or a dollar. In many instances, the amounts represented a huge sacrifice for the donors. One donation of a dollar was accompanied by the description, "An Old Man's Day's Wages." The aliases preferred by many donors revealed their feelings about the case. "Two fathers," each of whom gave a dollar, probably had daughters about Carrie's age. Others who signed themselves "an English working girl," or "one who knows," readily sympathized with Carrie's plight. For them, she had become a symbol of the abuses many young women faced every day in the workplace.

Even without financial backing, Carrie would have been able to choose from a wide selection of lawyers. Members of the legal profession were scrambling to become involved in a case that was shaping up to be one of the most sensational trials of the decade. But Carrie's brother-in-law had hired a Mr. Maw as soon as he heard about the shooting. He was determined to stay with this first choice, recommended to him by co-workers. As it turned out, Maw turned the case over to another member of his legal firm, Hartley Dewart, KC. Ironically, Dewart was the same lawyer who had helped prosecute Clara Ford ten years earlier after the shooting of another rich Torontonian, Frank Westwood.

On February 24, Carrie was indicted in a courtroom at Toronto City Hall. Escorted by a police matron and a Salvation Army worker, she seemed composed, smiling briefly as she entered the room. Dewart entered a plea of not guilty on her behalf. Then he and Crown Prosecutor E.E.A. Du Vernet discussed the trial date.

The assizes, which were already underway, had dragged on two weeks longer than expected. Jury members were tired and wanted to go home. There was also some concern that it might be difficult to find a judge to hear Carrie's case. However, if the jurors were dismissed, Carrie would have to wait until April, when the next assizes were scheduled. After some discussion, the presiding judge, Chief Justice William Mulock, agreed to hear the case. Carrie's trial was set for the morning of Friday, February 26.

From the first report of the shooting, scarcely a day had gone by without some aspect of the case being discussed in the Toronto papers. The details were well known and there was no doubt in anyone's mind that Carrie Davis had killed Bert Massey. The crucial question was whether or not she had been justified in doing so. Crown Prosecutor Du Vernet, knowing that public sympathy was on Carrie's side, made sure to praise her for her sense of duty and her attempt to seek help from her sister and brother-in-law. But the question remained. Had provocation been sufficient to make her lose control of herself, sufficient to induce such a state of fear, that the court might justifiably reduce the offence with which she was charged?

Most of the witnesses called by the prosecution focused on the details of the shooting and Carrie's behaviour. While he wisely refrained from slurs on her character, Du Vernet tried to convince the court that Carrie had overreacted to an incident that had not really caused her any lasting harm.

Carrie's attorney, Hartley Dewart, called only three witnesses — Dr. Beemer from the mental asylum, Carrie's brother-in-law Edmond Fairchild, and Carrie herself.

Fairchild corroborated Carrie's version of events on the Sunday afternoon when she had fled to his house. He also provided a vivid portrait of Carrie's upbringing. His wife and her sisters had been very strictly raised. They were expected to be obedient, were not allowed to speak unless spoken to, and their social life was closely supervised. When he was courting Carrie's older sister, Fairchild recalled, the girls were allowed out only two nights a week, and had to be home by nine o'clock.

Under cross-examination Fairchild also talked about Carrie's illness the previous summer. When he visited Carrie, Bert Massey told him that his sister-in-law would get the very best care possible. Her employer said he was "interested" in the girl. Massey reassured Fairchild that he and his wife could look after Carrie, and that Rhoda would "see that Carrie did not keep bad company." That, Fairchild commented, "threw him off."

Carrie was the last witness called. Modestly dressed in a dark brown coat and black velvet hat trimmed with ostrich feathers, she was pale and had apparently been crying. Two women supported her as she was placed in the prisoner's dock. When she took the stand, Chief Justice Mulock gave her permission to sit down. Carrie bravely replied that she could just as well stand. Again she told her story, although by now it was familiar to everyone in the courtroom.

The two lawyers then made their summations. Du Vernet argued that Carrie had used excessive force, and that Bert Massey had been killed for an offence that would have brought a six-month jail term. Carrie had overreacted, and would have been far wiser to stay away from the Massey house if she felt so strongly about her employer's advances.

Hartley Dewart painted a very different picture. Carrie was a good, decent girl, strictly brought up, obedient, careful of her reputation. She had taken on much of the responsibility for supporting her family and would not leave a well-paying position without careful consideration. She had made a promise to Mrs. Massey, one that she wanted to keep to the best of her ability. But she also knew Bert Massey was a determined man, considerably larger and more powerful than she. There had been no pre-meditation in her action of self-defence. Carrie had acted out of terror — not in fear for her life, but in fear for her chastity, which was as precious as life itself to a respectable woman.

The jury had three options: convict Carrie of murder, convict her of manslaughter, or set her free. However, Dewart argued, in view of Massey's behaviour, "It was not manslaughter; it was brute-slaughter."

In a long and poignant speech, Dewart also called up patriotic images — of Carrie waiting patiently for her soldier sweetheart, and the duty of Canadian men to protect the women of the British Empire.

> *Look the facts in the face. You have a wife, a daughter, or perhaps a sister at home. Can you look them squarely in the face, with a clear conscience, and say you did your duty upon the facts in this case if you leave a stain upon this girl by your verdict? Put any one of your own in this girl's position and think what you would say if a jury found them guilty on [sic] the same set of circumstances.*

By the time Hartley Dewart was finished, many listeners were weeping. The jury reached their decision in 30 minutes, and at 12:15 they rendered their verdict: Not Guilty. Nearly every man in the courtroom rose and cheered, creating such an uproar that Chief Justice Mulock nearly fell off his chair. Never before in his long years on the bench and he heard such a response.

Carrie was pale and trembling. As constables tried to restore order, she was helped from the prisoner's dock to the waiting arms of her sister. One of the constables went over to them and whispered, "She has not been freed yet." He led her back to the box. Carrie took a sip of water, composed herself, and waited. When he could finally make himself heard, Judge Mulock addressed her, saying that although the jury had taken an unconventional approach to the case, he completely agreed with their decision.

> *You have had a very strict bringing up, and the influence of your parents has fallen upon good ground. You entertained the highest regard for your honor and morality. These qualities in you caused you to take a stronger view of what Mr. Massey would have done than the facts warranted, but nevertheless, your education, training, and nature were such as to fill with alarm ... therefore, from the highest motives you did a thing which you will regret, perhaps, all your life ... You did it from a sense of duty. It was a mistaken way.*

Instead, the judge advised, she should have stayed out of the Massey house. He also commented on Carrie's motivation to fulfill the duties given her by Mrs. Massey. "So, trying to do your duty under all these circumstances you found yourself in this tragedy." By now, the judge had tears in his eyes.

"You are free to go now."

Carrie choked out a reply. "Thank you, judge. And thank you, gentlemen, who have tried me."

Carrie once again joined her sister. Together, they left the courtroom, got into a waiting automobile, and drove off in the direction of Morley Avenue. Her brief, traumatic time in the public eye had come to an end. With little apparent regret, and with her life returned to her, Carrie Davis disappeared into the obscurity of a working-class woman's life.

Chapter 8

Tessie Talley: "I Wish Emmett Talley's Soul Was in Hell"

S oon after the World War I, tobacco men from the southern United States began moving into southwestern Ontario, lured by the new agricultural trend of flue-cured tobacco, which would bring prosperity to farmers along the north shore of Lake Erie.

For years, Ontario farmers had been struggling to make a decent living on the light, sandy soil of the region. Some had grown tobacco for generations, but seldom in great quantity and rarely as their main crop. Around that time, North Carolinians had perfected a method for curing tobacco by slowly heating the green leaves in a wood-fired kiln until they turned a golden brown. The result was a milder, more desirable product.

But it required skill to produce a good tobacco crop — skill almost no one in Ontario possessed. Eventually, experienced tobacco workers from North Carolina, Virginia, and the adjoining states found their way to southwestern Ontario, where they helped out area farmers. Some went back to the States as soon as harvest was over. Others, gambling that the burgeoning tobacco industry would bring considerable prosperity to Ontario, decided to remain in Canada.

Emmett Talley was one of those who stayed. He had come from his native Virginia to southern Ontario along with his wife, Tessie, their children, and Tessie's parents, William and Lucy Tillotson. After spending some time in the Leamington area, Emmett and his extended family moved to Norfolk County. By 1927 they were settled in Delhi, about an hour southwest of London.

Emmett Talley was a good worker and a loving father. But he had a number of personality problems. Henry Mauthe, who worked for him, described him as a man who "got discouraged easily." He was also rough with horses, the animals that powered most of the equipment then used on Ontario farms. But Henry hesitated to describe Emmett as bad-tempered.

Possibly Emmett was pleasant enough when dealing with men, or even with women outside his own family circle. He certainly seemed to enjoy the company of the drinking buddies who frequently showed up at his house, as they sat for hours, talking and swigging moonshine whiskey.

Prohibition had more or less come to an end in Ontario in early 1927 with the establishment of the Liquor Control Board of Ontario. On June 1 of that year, the first government liquor stores opened. It was now possible to purchase alcohol legally if you were over 21 and had a permit. But the permit could be revoked if, in the opinion of liquor store staff, you were drinking too much.

Emmett had a reputation as a heavy drinker, so it was only a matter of time before liquor store staff cut off his supply. Just how much he drank was open to question. Some of his acquaintances said he was intoxicated at least three times a week. Others claimed they had often seen him drinking, but had never seen him drunk. But several willingly attested to a dramatic change in his personality — and especially in the way he treated his wife — when he was drinking.

It was all a moot point for Emmett, who had continued to drink even during Prohibition. He found it just as easy to continue relying on bootleggers, a number of whom were still doing a brisk business in the Delhi vicinity.

Ross Jones and W.H. Hamilton went to the Talley house for dinner on May 1, 1927. Emmett had been drinking before they arrived but, Jones thought, was not drunk. Still, he and Tessie were fighting when their guests arrived. According to Jones, Emmett had "thrown his wife down and was beating her." By the time Hamilton pulled them apart Emmett had pulled out some of Tessie's hair, given her a black eye, smashed one of her teeth, and broken the skin on her throat.

Jones and Hamilton probably said very little to Emmett about the brawl. What went on between a man and his wife was really none of their business. Besides, according to Emmett, Tessie and her mother were always nagging him about his drinking. In fact, he claimed, Tessie could be "as mean as a devil, and wanted to run everything her own way." Sometimes Emmett even agreed with the women, conceding that he could do better, and that he wanted to raise his three children properly. But his good intentions were usually forgotten as soon as he started drinking.

On Saturday, July 30, 1927, Tessie and Emmett went out for an evening. Tessie was ready to head home around midnight. Emmett, who'd once again had too much to drink, wanted to keep partying. A couple of friends were waiting in their car, ready to head over to the bootlegger's and get another bottle. As Tessie tried to talk him out of it, Emmett grew angry. Soon, both were yelling in the street. Emmett swore and shoved Tessie, sending her into the ditch at the side of the road before staggering off to meet his friends.

Herman Atkins heard the angry voices outside his house, then the sound of Tessie crying. He went outside to see what was going on. Tessie was an acquaintance, so Atkins asked her if she would like to come inside. Tessie accepted the invitation.

Atkins probably realized Tessie needed another woman to calm her down, so he sent her upstairs to sit with his housekeeper, Annie Vogel. Tessie was shaken and still furious from the altercation. "I wish Emmett Talley's soul was in hell and I had the receipt for it," she told Annie. A little later Atkins took Tessie to a coffee shop where they chatted briefly. At one point Tessie said she was thinking of having Emmett arrested.

Atkins suggested she call her father and have him drive her home. Tessie did so, but she probably said nothing about what had happened earlier that evening. Bill Tillotson knew his daughter and son-in-law quarrelled frequently, but he wasn't aware that their fights had ever become physical.

The next day was Sunday. After sleeping off the effects of Saturday night, Emmett was ready for another round of drinks. Several men dropped by the Talley house that afternoon, including Henry Abbott, William Wilson, and Tessie's father. By six o'clock that evening they'd gone through a quart of moonshine whiskey. Emmett wanted more, so Wilson went off to get another bootlegged bottle. When he returned, Wilson had one drink from the bottle then said goodbye. Emmett continued to drink, and Tessie decided to go to bed.

Around eleven o'clock she was suddenly awakened. Emmett was moving around, choking and vomiting into the slop bucket by the back door. He had endured episodes like this in the past, typically brought on by too much drinking, but this one seemed more serious than the others. In between spasms, he called to her and the children.

Scrambling out of bed, Tessie went to Emmett. He asked her to get her parents and a doctor. She immediately telephoned Dr. E.W. Zumstein. He was out, so his wife took the message. But between Tessie's excitement and her North Carolinian accent, the doctor's wife wasn't quite sure what the problem was.

Leaving Emmett and the children in the house, Tessie hurried out to the car to drive to her parents' house. As she passed the storefronts in the centre of town, Tessie spotted two acquaintances, Henry Birdsall and Courtney Smith. She stopped long enough to tell them something was seriously wrong with Emmett and asked them to go to the house and stay with him and the children. Then she continued on her way while Birdsall went to see what he could do for Emmett. He found the stricken man lying on his bed, half dressed, with a child on either side of him. The two little girls were trying to keep him from falling on the floor during his convulsions.

Tessie and her mother arrived a few minutes later. "Mama's here," Tessie told her husband. "Ah ha," was Emmett's only response. Finally, Dr. Zumstein arrived. It had been less than 20 minutes since Tessie summoned him.

When his wife had relayed the message, Zumstein had assumed it was a simple case of choking. Now, as he briefly examined Emmett, other possibilities came to mind. He questioned Tessie. Yes, she told him, he'd had episodes like this before, but never as violent as this one. Leaving Tessie and the others to watch the patient, Zumstein slipped out to get something from his office and to call in Dr. R.B. Hare of Simcoe to consult with him.

By the time he returned, Emmett was dead.

Tessie looked stunned. Then she burst into tears. It was the moonshine that had killed her husband, she said, as she handed the doctor the bottle Emmett had been drinking from. Dr. Zumstein took the bottle, which was nearly full, but said nothing to confirm Tessie's suspicions. He had a theory of his own: Emmett's symptoms had all the earmarks of strychnine poisoning.

He alerted Coroner Robert Tisdale. Zumstein and Dr. Hare analyzed the contents of the bottle. They found nothing unusual, but their hunch that Emmett had been poisoned was so strong they decided an autopsy was necessary. Tessie objected, saying she did not want her husband cut up, but there was nothing she could do. The autopsy proceeded and Emmett's stomach was sent to Toronto for analysis. When the report came back, Dr. Zumstein's suspicions were confirmed. The provincial analyst had found 1.5 grains of strychnine in Emmett's stomach, more than enough to kill a man.

Meanwhile, Tessie was trying to come to grips with her loss. The morning after Emmett's death, she and her mother worked together in the Talley house, making funeral preparations. As they cleaned, they threw some scraps into the slop bucket. They also dumped in the two inches of whiskey remaining in the glass Emmett had used the night before. A little later, Henry Mauthe, the hired hand threw the contents of the bucket — including Emmett's vomit from the night before — to the pigs. Within moments of swallowing the swill, one pig started to squeal and jump around. Mauthe reported the strange behaviour to Tessie, who thought the animal was simply very hungry. Then one of the pigs collapsed and died. Another started to behave strangely. Mauthe got some castor oil from the house and dosed the pig, but the remedy failed. The second pig also died. Again, Tessie blamed the moonshine.

She stuck to that story when she took Emmett's body home to Clarkson, Virginia, telling her brother-in-law that poisoned moonshine had been the cause of death. Meanwhile, back in Ontario, officials arrested John Koluk, the bootlegger who had provided the whiskey.

On August 15 an inquest into the death of Emmett Talley opened in the jam-packed Delhi Town Hall. Rumours had been flying through the community and everyone wanted to see what witnesses had to say about the circumstances of Talley's death. By the time proceedings began they had something else to talk about. Tessie did not appear at the inquest, saying she was too ill to attend.

Along with testimony about the Talleys' stormy relationship, witnesses recounted the details of Emmett's last days. They also reported on Tessie's behaviour before and after his death, with some of the most damning information coming from Annie Vogel, the woman who had comforted her after the Saturday night fight in front of Herman Atkins' house. According to Annie, after Emmett's death Tessie started visiting her regularly. Up to that point, she said, they had never really been friendly. After all, being only 21, Annie was 10 years younger than Tessie. As she described their conversations, she revealed that shortly after Emmett died Tessie had asked her not to repeat the comment about wishing her husband was in hell.

Medical testimony confirmed that Emmett had died of strychnine poisoning. The big questions were, "Where had it come from?" and "How had it been administered?" Tessie's mother, Lucy Tillotson, provided some of the answers.

At first she denied any knowledge of strychnine. She said Emmett had talked about poisoning an old dog that was hanging around his farm and disturbing the hens when they were laying eggs. She had no idea whether he had actually done anything about it, although the dog was no longer around. Lucy also admitted that in North Carolina she had once put out two tablets of strychnine to poison a dog, which had died on her verandah.

Crown Attorney William E. Kelly asked if she had ever bought strychnine in Canada. Lucy denied it. With a flourish, Kelly produced a document bearing the signature L.V. Tillotson and handed it to her. Lucy Veturia Tillotson slowly removed her hat, put on her glasses, and peered at the paper. Yes, she admitted, the signature was hers.

"Would it surprise you to be told that the document is a receipt for strychnine?" Kelly asked. Dated February 24, 1927, it had been issued by Willoughby's drugstore in Leamington.

"Oh, I remember," Lucy said. "That was strychnine we

got to kill that old dog."

When Kelly asked why had she denied purchasing strychnine, Lucy replied, "I just forgot."

Lucy Tillotson was not the most credible witness. Not only had she "forgotten" about buying strychnine, she had also testified that Tessie had never been in any kind of trouble before. In fact, Tessie had been involved in a lawsuit in the United States. Although the details were irrelevant to the poisoning case, Lucy's misrepresentation of the facts made her testimony unreliable. It was easy for spectators and officers of the court to conclude she would go to almost any lengths to protect her daughter.

Several witnesses testified that Emmett was sometimes despondent and, when drunk, often stated he thought he was going to die. Although there were hints that he might have been suicidal, nothing conclusive was presented to the court.

Between adjournments and other delays, the verdict of the coroner's jury was not rendered until September 12. Their decision was straightforward: "We find that Emmett Talley came to his death in the Township of Windham on August 1st, 1927, by strychnine poisoning, how or by whom administered we do not know."

As far as the authorities were concerned, the jury's decision was far from satisfactory. With no strong evidence that Emmett had committed suicide, the only other option was that someone had poisoned him. John Koluk, the bootlegger who provided Emmett's last bottle of whiskey, was off the hook — guilty of nothing more than liquor law violations. But Tessie, who had eventually returned from Virginia, remained a suspect.

On Tuesday, September 27, police constable Harold Hough and inspector Albert Wood called at the Talley residence. When Tessie opened the door, they announced that they had come to arrest her. Stunned but compliant, Tessie asked to be allowed to take her three-year-old daughter to her mother's house. The policemen consented and accompanied her to the Tillotsons, where Tessie also made arrangements for the care of her two school-aged daughters. Then she went with Hough and Wood to the Norfolk County Jail.

Tessie's preliminary hearing took place in October. Although there was no new evidence, what was presented persuaded the jury that Tessie should be sent to trial. Arguments that alcohol poisoning might have caused Emmett's death were overturned by medical testimony about strychnine and its effects. Lucy Tillotson's purchase of the poison proved that strychnine was available. As to motive, there were two possibilities. Crown Attorney W.E. Kelly made a futile attempt to persuade the jurors that Tessie might have been involved with someone else. She was more than a decade younger than her husband, attractive enough, and men were always coming and going at the Talley house. But none of the Talleys' friends or acquaintances would corroborate Kelley's theory. Certainly there were plenty of male visitors, but there was no evidence of jealousy on Emmett's part or any kind of extra-marital involvement on Tessie's.

The strongest motive Tessie had for killing her husband was to escape his physical abuse. As Annie Vogel testified, Tessie had been angry enough to wish that he were dead after the fight in front of Herman Atkins's house. What went through her mind when Emmett hit her, blackened her eye, or broke her teeth? Today, defence lawyers would focus on the physical abuse Tessie had suffered, arguing that if she had killed Emmett she had done so out of fear for her life. But battered wives accused of murder could not fall back on self-defence in the 1920s. In fact, Emmett's treatment of Tessie just strengthened the Crown's case, providing her with a very strong motive for poisoning him.

The preliminary hearing ended on October 12, 1927, with a decision to send Tessie to trial for murder. Tessie was returned to her cell to wait until February. Six days later, she sent for Harold Hough, one of the policemen who had arrested her. When he arrived, she made a startling revelation. She'd had two dreams. In one, her father had been in a car accident. In the other, she had found a letter from Emmett lying under a napkin in her dining room. Would Hough go and look for it?

Hough, who had searched the house thoroughly in August, was skeptical. But Tessie was so persuasive that he gave in. He contacted her father, and he and Bill Tillotson went to the Talley house. There was no letter under a napkin, but there was one under a doily on a china cabinet.

Signed by Emmett, it read: "Tessie, don't wory [*sic*] about me, am sorry about last night. Will never be here to do it again; keep the kids with you and don't let no one have them. Take me back to old Virginia and you go with me and carry the kids with you. I wish we had have gone when we were talking about it and I have decided to go and stay."

There was more: instructions about paying Henry Mauthe what was owed, and how to handle the tobacco crop. Emmett ended the letter, "with love to all."

Tessie's murder trial opened on February 7, 1928. By this time, interest in the case had spread throughout Ontario and reporters from the Toronto newspapers were out in full force to cover the proceedings. So were a large number of women who crowded into the courtroom to watch the last act in the Talleys' domestic drama unfold.

Tessie entered the courtroom wearing a black silk coat trimmed with fur, a white scarf, and a close-fitting black hat. She took her place in the prisoner's dock and removed the coat. Underneath she was wearing a black dress with a single white artificial flower pinned on the left shoulder. Tessie watched carefully as each juror entered the room. Throughout the proceedings she occasionally glanced at her mother, who sat among the spectators with one of Tessie's daughters. Most of the time, her face was expressionless, as though the events being discussed had nothing to do with her.

Except for the letter that had surfaced after Tessie's

unusual dream, all the evidence had already been discussed at the inquest and preliminary hearing. The letter proved inconclusive. O.B. Stanton, a Toronto handwriting expert, testified that he had compared the so-called suicide note with a letter written by Emmett to his brother. As far as Stanton was concerned, the note found by Hough in the Talley dining room had not been written by the same person. But he also added that his opinion was "not always absolutely correct."

At 11:45 on the morning of February 8, the Crown wrapped up its case. Victor T. Foley, Tessie's lawyer, rose and addressed the court. As far as he was concerned, there was no need for the defence to proceed — the prosecution's case, based almost exclusively on circumstantial evidence, was too weak to convince anyone that murder had been committed.

Judge Rose reflected a moment, agreed there was not very much evidence, and then turned the matter over to the jury. It was up to them, he instructed, to decide whether they wanted to hear more evidence. He also advised them to consider one crucial question. "Could any reasonable man say that anything had been said in evidence to connect this woman with the crime?"

The jury withdrew and returned less than 20 minutes later. They did not need to hear further evidence, the foreman announced. There was no proof that Tessie Talley was responsible for her husband's death. The judge thanked the jury, expressing his own opinion that they had reached the right conclusion. Tessie was told she could go free.

Foley walked over to Tessie to congratulate her. She barely acknowledged him. As she stepped down from the dock, her mother pushed her way forward, took her by the arm, and walked with her out of the courtroom.

The letter found in the Talley dining room suggested that Emmett and Tessie had talked about returning to the south. Tessie never did return, at least not permanently. She spent the remainder of her life in Norfolk County, where she died in December 1970.

Further Reading

Marjorie Freeman Campbell. *Torso: The Evelyn Dick Case*. Toronto: Macmillan of Canada, 1974.

Cheryl MacDonald. *Who Killed George? The Ordeal of Olive Sternaman*. Toronto: Natural Heritage/Natural History, Inc., 1994.

Acknowledgements

Special thanks go to Kimberly Hurst, UE, for access to the London family papers, and to my editor, Deborah Lawson.

Quoted material used in this book was drawn from the following published sources:

Felons of Norfolk by John Ayre (1997), privately published;

Women on the Gallows by Frank W. Anderson (1987), privately published;

Canadian Freeman;

Dictionary of Canadian Biography;

Globe (Toronto, Ontario);

Hamilton Spectator;

London Free Press;

Niagara Herald;

Sault Star (Sault Ste. Marie, Ontario);

Simcoe Reformer;

St. Catharines Constitutional;

Toronto Evening Telegram;

Weekly British Whig (Kingston, Ontario);

Woodstock Sentinel.

Dubinsky, Karen and Franca Iacovetta. "Murder, Womanly Virtue and Motherhood: The Case of Angelina Napolitano, 1911–1922." *Canadian Historical Review.* LXXII 4, 1991.

Strange, Carolyn. "Wounded Womanhood and Dead Men: Chivalry and the Trials of Clara Ford and Carrie Davis. *Gender Conflicts: New Essays in Women's History.*

About the Author

Cheryl MacDonald has been writing about Canadian history for nearly 30 years. A long-time resident of Nanticoke, Ontario, she is a full-time writer and historian whose weekly history column appears in the *Simcoe Times-Reformer*. Her historical articles have appeared in *The Beaver, Maclean's,* tho *Hamilton Spectator,* and *The Old Farmer's Almanac.* Cheryl has written more than 20 books on Canadian and Ontario history, including Amazing Stories titles *Niagara Daredevils, Great Canadian Love Stories,* and *Christmas in Ontario.* Currently completing a master's degree in history at McMaster University, Hamilton, Cheryl MacDonald can be contacted through her website: www.heronwoodent.ca

TRUE CANADIAN
AMAZING STORIES™

ONTARIO MURDERS

Mysteries, Scandals, and
Dangerous Criminals

CRIME/MYSTERY

by Susan McNicoll

ONTARIO MURDERS
Mysteries, Scandals, and Dangerous Criminals

"From an early age, lying came easily to her. Everything she did was a performance, a role she played to create an illusion."

Six chilling stories of notorious Ontario murders are recounted in this spine-tingling collection. From the pretty but dangerous Evelyn Dick to the mysterious murder of one of the Fathers of Confederation, Thomas D'Darcy McGee, these stories will keep you on the edge of your seat.

 True stories. Truly Canadian.

ISBN 1-55153-951-9

BRITISH COLUMBIA MURDERS
Mysteries, Crimes, and Scandals

"More than 30 wounds had been dug into her body with a knife... For more than 50 years, the police would be virtually certain who her murderer was, but would never charge him. Why?"

Lock your doors and draw your curtains... Six of British Columbia's most notorious murders are recounted in these gripping stories of betrayal and intrigue. From the tragic murder of Molly Justice to the unsolved mystery of Janet Smith's untimely death, these stories will keep you on the edge of your seat.

 True stories. Truly Canadian.

ISBN 1-55153-963-2

PRAIRIE MURDERS
Mysteries, Crimes, and Scandals

*"The devil told me to kill Martin Sitar
and all his family, and then go
away and hide in the bushes."*
Mass-murderer Thomas Hreshkoski

Seven chilling stories of murders across the Prairies are recounted in this gripping collection. Not for the faint-hearted, these stories tell of violence and bloodshed, as well as the police investigations that led to the eventual capture of the perpetrators. From the "Ductman of Drumheller" to the murder of Banff cabbie Lucie Turmel, these true stories will keep you on the edge of your seat.

 True stories. Truly Canadian.

ISBN 1-55439-050-8

OTHER AMAZING STORIES

These titles are available wherever you buy books. If you have trouble finding the book you want, call the Altitude order desk at **1-800-957-6888**, e-mail your request to: **orderdesk@altitudepublishing.com** or visit our Web site at **www.amazingstories.ca**

New **AMAZING STORIES** titles are published every month.